Louisiana
DAYRIDE

52
SHORT TRIPS
FROM
NEW ORLEANS

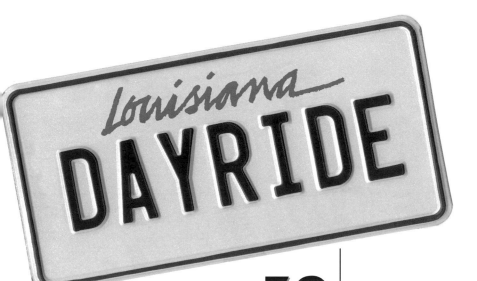

Louisiana DAYRIDE

52
SHORT TRIPS
FROM
NEW ORLEANS

Written and Illustrated by
Shelley N. C. Holl

University
Press
of
Mississippi
Jackson

To my husband: writer, editor and critic
Chris Waddington
for your unflagging confidence, rock-sure eye,
and that weekly professional massage.
The next book is yours.

Manufactured in
the United States

Designed by
Williams and Williams, Inc.

Many of the stories
in this book were first
published in slightly different
form in the Lagniappe section
of *The Times-Picayune*
newspaper.

Library of Congress
Cataloging in-Publication Data
Holl, Shelley N. C.
Louisiana dayride : 52 short trips
from New Orleans / by Shelley
N. C. Holl ; with illustrations and
photographs by the author.
        p.   cm.
Includes index.
ISBN 0-87805-822-2 (alk. paper)
1. New Orleans Region (La.)—
Guidebooks. 2. Louisiana—
Guidebooks. 3. Mississippi—
Guidebooks. I. Title.
F379.N53H65 1995
917.63'350463—dc20
95-31370
CIP
British Cataloging in-
Publication Data available

52 SHORT TRIPS FROM NEW ORLEANS

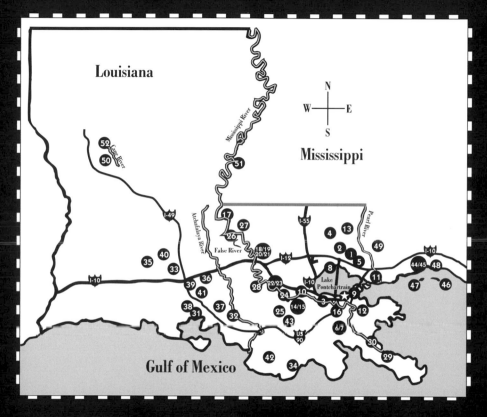

Contents

TRIPS OF ONE TO TWO HOURS
Downriver

TRIPS OF ONE TO THREE HOURS
Cajun Country

TRIPS OF ONE TO TWO HOURS
Mississippi

TRIPS OF THREE TO FOUR HOURS

Preface

In 1992 I took a deep breath and moved from the upper reaches of the Mississippi River to its outlet in Louisiana—a distance of over twelve hundred miles that barely seemed to account for the sudden change I experienced in climate, landscape, and culture. I had always wanted to live in a foreign land, and I found one without even leaving the lower forty-eight states!

I was still surrounded by shipping boxes when a *Times-Picayune* editor asked me to write a travel column of short trips for "Lagniappe," the paper's weekly entertainment section. I decided to try it, thinking that a little travelling might help me get my bearings. Ten thousand miles later, I am still finding fascinating new places to visit just a few hours drive from New Orleans—and wondering whether this would have worked in any other area. South Louisiana and the Mississippi Gulf Coast are a dream for any traveler who prefers a cultural collage to synthetic tourist attractions.

This book is based on first-hand reporting and on-site sketches made during two years of weekly trips. The main stories all appeared in slightly different form in my "L'Attitude" column in *The Times-Picayune*, but extra information and side trips have been added.

HOW TO USE THIS BOOK

Louisiana Dayride is a starting point for travelers who want to participate in the many cultures of the Gulf South, instead of merely observing them on a tour. One of the things I've grown to love about Louisianians and our neighbors in Mississippi is that almost everyone is willing to stop and talk. The people of these states are the real travel attractions. Whether talking to a Coushatta Indian, a Creole sugarcane planter, or a Cajun ship builder, I found genuine warmth and heard life stories different from those of most Americans. If you take the opportunity to say hello, you will find the same things.

Louisiana Dayride is organized by one-way travel time and direction from New Orleans. If you wish to travel upriver, downriver, into Cajun country, or Mississippi you can turn to the appropriate section and find many destinations in the same general area. Within each section, the trips are arranged alphabetically by location. For most locations, several side trips in the area are given.

To prepare for day trips in any season, I bring rain gear, mosquito repellent, suntan lotion, boots, and drinking water whether I'm staying in swampy southern Louisiana or heading for the rolling wooded countryside of Mississippi. I used to bring lunch from New Orleans until someone told me that "food is the only real religion in Louisiana." Now I try cafes and markets everywhere, and my best discoveries are included in the book.

Most of the activities included are inexpensive. Prices and hours of operation are subject to change, so you should plan to call in advance. General pricing guidelines per person are indicated as follows:

$ = $5 and under $$$ = $11-20
$$ = $10 and under $$$$ = $20 and up

Many friends helped with this book—first among them the people of Louisiana and Mississippi who opened their homes and businesses to me and took time to answer the questions of a transplanted Yankee from New Orleans. Long days and drives were eased by adventurous friends who joined me on these trips.

The manuscript owes much to my husband, Chris Waddington, writer *extraordinaire* who first edited the columns then helped me transform them into a book. My writing also benefitted from close attention by editors at *The Times-Picayune*: Renée Peck, Karen Taylor-Gist and Jonathan Perrow. Julia Nead, Richard Dodds, Millie Ball, and other colleagues at the *Picayune* took a special interest in this project. Authors Andrei Codrescu and Randolph Delehanty both offered professional advice at a crucial moment. Much

thanks to Julia McSherry for copy editing, to Noah Robert for guidance, Donna Perret for business acumen, and to Justine McCarthy for her moral support and good humor. Robert and Phyllis O'Hair loaned me art equipment and expertise. Joe Arrigo and Jean and Charlotte Seidenberg helped me through the maze of publishing. Finally a special thanks to JoAnne Prichard of University Press of Mississippi who took a chance with a first-time author.

TRIPS WITHIN ONE HOUR

Abita Brewing Company & Country Fun

BREWING A SMALL TOWN CURE FOR URBAN BLUES

HOW TO GO:
Take the Causeway north across Lake Pontchartrain to I-12 east, then north on Hwy. 59 to Abita Springs. Turn left at the Abita Brewing Company gift shop, cross the Tammany Trace. Turn left, then go straight to the Abita Springs Tourist Park.

BEST TIMES TO GO:
When the weather cooperates.

ABITA BREWING COMPANY
21084 Hwy. 36
Covington, LA
(504) 893-3143

Tours at 1 PM
Check at the gift shop in Abita Springs first and get directions to the new plant, 1.2 miles west of town on the Covington Abita Highway.

ABITA SPRINGS CAFE
22132 Level Street
Abita Springs, LA 70420
(504) 867-9950

Mon. Tues. Sun. 8 AM - 3 PM
Wed. closed
Thurs.
8 AM - 8 PM
Fri. Sat.
8 AM - 9 PM

Abita Brewing Company—one of the fastest growing micro-breweries in the United States—uses the same artesian waters that once drew health seekers and Native Americans to the North Shore community.

City life getting you down? Take a tip from turn-of-the-century doctors who prescribed trips to Abita Springs for fresh air and spring water cures. The modern cure—a country style breakfast at the Abita Springs Cafe, a stroll among the Victorian cottages of Abita's old town, a bike ride beneath the towering pines on the Tammany Trace, or an hour-long tour of the Abita Brewing Company—draws families from throughout the area every weekend.

Abita's pure artesian well water makes it the perfect site for one of the nation's fastest growing micro-breweries. Eighteen months ago I looked for the home of the frothy Turbo Dog beer and found the original site of the Abita Brewing Company in a pair of garage-like buildings in the center of town. Now only the gift shop is left on the site—a brew pub will be built there soon—and the manufacturing operation has moved a mile out of town to a much larger facility. Tours, accompanied by generous tastes of the brew, are offered each Saturday at 1:00 p.m. Visitors can follow the entire brewing process, starting with a taste of the raw materials, such as imported malt and wheat, and ending with a sip of such experimental brews as Purple Haze or a potent barley wine.

Another newcomer in town is the Abita Springs Cafe. Veteran restaurateur, Sandi Cerise, has applied her experience at several New Orleans eateries to the creation of a quintessential country cafe: breakfast all day on Saturday and Sunday, ice pops for the kids, and local artist Bunny Matthew's handiwork all over the beaded board walls.

While families on bikes arrived from morning rides on the nearby Tammany Trace, I sat on the cafe's front porch sipping ice tea and sketching the gleaming white steeple of Trinity Evangelical Lutheran Church. Around me diners sampled omelettes, po' boys with home cooked roast beef and other goodies. I topped off my visit with a slice of Cerise's specialty pizza made from cookie dough and fresh fruit. Smiling with pride, she sweetened her confection with a bit of tableside talk: "I thought about retiring but fell in love with this building and this town," she said. "From the kitchen I can hear church bells ringing. Then the people come over with their families. This is a real nice small town."

NEARBY — TAMMANY TRACE

The Trace is an old railroad bed that's been converted to a bicycling, walking, and equestrian trail. At this writing nine of a total thirty-one miles have been completed.

Entrance points are located in Abita Springs at Trace Headquarters in Mandeville - 1/2 mile north of I-12 on Highway 59 on the left.

ABITA QUAIL FARM

If you have a yen for exotic cooking, try ordering a dozen quail from the La Ferme de Caille (Abita Quail Farm). Phone ahead for quail that is plainly dressed, partially deboned, or deboned and stuffed with wild rice. The prices are quite reasonable. But the real treat is driving on Highway 36 to pick up the quail. The Abita Quail Farm is a picturesque wedding folly complete with peacocks, reflecting pond, horses, and a fully equipped catering kitchen. When I visited, owner Jack Hines was stuffing a pig with jambalaya to be carried in flaming on a landau for a New Year's party. Julia Childs once made the trip to La Ferme de Caille just to witness the torching.

Trinity Evangelical Lutheran Church as seen from the Abita Springs Cafe, a picturesque lunch stop along the Tammany Trace bike path.

ABITA QUAIL FARM
23185 Hwy. 435
Abita Springs, LA
(504) 892-5176
Available for weddings, banquets, and other catered gatherings.

HOW TO GO:
Follow Hwy. 435 (Level Street) northeast out of Abita Springs to reach the Abita Quail Farm.

WHAT'S A TURBO DOG?

Abita Brewing Company owner Jim Patton claims, "We made a beer similar to one known as Old Brown Dog and didn't know what to call it. We tasted it and we knew there was no other possible name. I guess we knew we had something when I walked into Tipitina's during Jazz Fest and found half the customers standing on the bar barking."

Peacocks and swans roam the groomed lawns of the Abita Quail Farm. Locals recommend the stuffed and deboned quail for sale at the rural banqueting facility.

Artists' Haven

OLD TOWN NORTH OF LAKE PONTCHARTRAIN RICH IN DECORATIVE ARTS

HOW TO GO:

Causeway north across Lake Pontchartrain. Follow signs to U.S. 190 - Covington business district. This becomes Boston Street. Lee Lane crosses it just after you enter town. St. Tammany Art Museum: Left on New Hampshire, the museum is 2 1/2 blocks further.

ST. TAMMANY ART MUSEUM

129 North New Hampshire
Covington, LA
(504) 892-8650
Changing shows and directions to local galleries.

CHRIST EPISCOPAL CHURCH

(Across from St. Tammany Art Museum)
Covington, LA
(504) 892-3177

Early nineteenth-century structure with a quiet garden.

DO THE DISHES

434 Columbia Street
Covington, LA
(504) 893-3873

Decorating your own dinnerware is fun for both kids and adults.

BOAT FESTIVAL

The Madisonville Wooden Boat Festival is held each year in September. Thousands of boat enthusiasts descend upon the little town of Madisonville to view wooden boats, join the Quick and Dirty Boat Building Contest, shop at the Marine Flea Market and enjoy food, workshops, parades, and sea trials. For more information call: (504) 898-2029.

S earching for a custom stone mantel, wrought iron garden benches, or gothic cross candlesticks big enough for an altar? All can be found in the craft workshops, studios, and galleries of Covington, the eye of a creative storm that's sweeping over Lake Pontchartrain's north shore.

I previewed the city's art riches in a day-long tour that took me from painting galleries to studios full of busy artisans cranking out orders for lamps, men's ties, and serving platters.

"Covington's strength is in the decorative arts," said Don Marshall, director of the St. Tammany Arts Association. "We have potters that have as many as six full-time workers."

Historically, Covington has always been a shopping center for north shore communities. Established in 1913, it was a port with a dock on the Bogue Falaya River and a railroad connection. As the parish seat, it had the courthouse, feed and seed stores, and groceries. The entire downtown area is on the National Register of Historic Places. Today

Artist Jane Boswell-Adams shows off a hand-painted ceramic lamp outside Fiasco, one of many thriving craft businesses in Covington.

specialty stores fill Lee Lane and the Market—shopping areas that bracket the old downtown area—and Covington's calendar lists festivals, gallery walks, and musical events. More than 50 antique dealers are located in town.

MADISONVILLE — A SIDE TRIP FOR BOAT LOVERS

Boats were everywhere in Madisonville, Louisiana: Masts poked up behind gas stations and cemetery crypts. The sounds of horns, shipbells, and outboard motors filled the air.

Sheltered by pines and paved in shells, the oldest permanent settlement in St. Tammany Parish occupies the west bank of the Tchefuncte River where it empties into Lake Pontchartrain. Its deep water port still attracts pleasure boaters and fishermen, just as it once brought ocean going vessels to the southern end of the Natchez Trace. Deck-loaded schooners bearing farm produce, lumber, and other goods sailed from Madisonville to New Orleans. Sailors relied on the flashing signal of Madisonville's historic lighthouse, visible for 11 miles across the treacherous waters of Lake

Pontchartrain. Today the lighthouse stands offshore and the road that once led to it dead ends into the lake, leaving me pining for a boat of my own.

Instead I walked through town, a pastel collection of raised cottages punctuated by a mansion and a small brick museum which displays Civil War weapons and Indian relics. The mansion houses Regent Square, an elegant interior decorating shop.

Later I stopped for an informal tour of the Madisonville Boat Yard with yard supervisor Leslie Fields and began to believe that everyone in Madisonville has a boat. "What makes our yard unique is that we work almost exclusively on wooden boats and we also allow families to come here and work on their own boats," he explained. Boat yards have occupied this site as long as anyone can remember. Large wooden boats—some longer than 200 feet—were made on the banks of the Tchefuncte. Many came to rest here too—more than 100 were scuttled in the river's deep holes to avoid repair bills or enemy capture during various wars.

A museum is proposed for a site adjacent to the Madisonville Boat Yard. According to museum proponents, Madisonville's Tchefuncte River is the richest cache of submerged and preserved antique boats in the country. But until they can raise the money—and the boats—visitors must content themselves with viewing more visible inventory. Wooden boats at the yard ranged from a sleek drug running cruiser (forcibly retired) to a vintage 1940s Coast Guard picket boat. Given this diversity, it's no surprise that boatyard workers responded with one voice when asked to suggest activities in Madisonville: "Rent a boat and get out on the water."

Wooden vessels fill the Tchefuncte River across from the historic Madisonville Boat Yard.

HOW TO GO:

Causeway north across Lake Pontchartrain to the exit for Mandeville. Left (west) under the bridge onto Hwy. 22. Follow Hwy. 22 until you cross the Tchefuncte River into Madisonville.

The Madisonville lighthouse can be seen from the end of Lake Road. Drive south on Main Street and keep going after it becomes Lake Road.

MADISONVILLE BOAT YARD

You'll pass the yard halfway to the lighthouse on the east side of the road. At the entrance is the old lightkeeper's house, moved from its original location next to the lighthouse in the 1940s.

MORTON'S

702 Water Street / Madisonville, LA
(504) 845-4970

Morton's is just to the left as you cross the bridge into Madisonville. It offers boiled seafood, a comfortable atmosphere, and a friendly bar.

MADISONVILLE MUSEUM

201 Cedar Street / (504) 845-2100

Open Saturdays and Sundays 10 AM - 4 PM. Tours by appointment.

FAIRVIEW RIVERSIDE STATE PARK

East bank of the Tchefuncte River. Turn right before crossing the bridge into town. Tent and trailer campsites, nature trails, and boat slips are available.

BOAT RENTAL

Boats can be rented at Salty's Marina on the east side of the Tchefuncte. If you can supply your own craft, a public boat launch is located on Lake Avenue in Madisonville and permits are available at City Hall.

Destrehan Plantation

AN EIGHTEENTH-CENTURY GEM JUST OUTSIDE NEW ORLEANS

HOW TO GO:
I-10 west to I-310. Take I-310 south to the Destrehan exit. At the end of the exit turn left beneath the bridge onto River Road. Destrehan is one-half mile beyond the bridge on the left.

BEST TIME TO GO:
Fewer tour buses in the morning.

DESTREHAN PLANTATION
P.O. Box 5
9999 River Road
Destrehan, LA 70047
(504) 764-9315
9:30 AM - 4 PM
Seven days
By admission: $$
Open 10:30 AM - 4 PM daily except major holidays. Last tour begins at 4 PM.

have been giving tours at Destrehan Plantation for several years, but today the house looks completely different than when I began because of all the furniture acquired from the family," said Lou Flanigan, tour guide at Destrehan.

As a first time visitor, everything at Destrehan Plantation was new to me, but I went with someone who could remember the house before renovation, standing empty and neglected amid a thicket of tangled undergrowth. The interior of the 1790s landmark was badly vandalized, and the marble fireplaces, doorknobs, and light fixtures had all been stolen. The local sheriff managed to stop thieves just as they were making off with a marble bathtub said to be a gift from Napoleon to the Destrehans.

Destrehan's video shows the vandalized property, but today the house has no visible damage. The grounds are well-tended and the house, though sparsely furnished in places, is once again a fitting home for a marble bathtub. One unrestored room lets you see beneath the plaster and lathe to the bousillage and hand-hewn cypress beams. There is also a model which shows how the twin garconniéres and back gallery were enclosed within the house during its remodeling to Greek Revival style in 1840. The house before remodeling reminded me of the raised Creole style of nearby Laura Plantation.

Once in ruins, Destrehan Plantation has been restored to the style of the 1840s by the River Road Historical Society.

Since 1971 the River Road Historical Society that saved Destrehan Plantation has been stabilizing the eighteenth-century Creole structure and restoring and furnishing it in 1840s style. Each year the society collects enough funds to purchase a few more furnishings from the family's descendants.

Several family portraits were added to the house in 1994 including that of Lydia Rost. Her portrait lets tour guides put a face to a family tragedy. She died in 1853 from yellow fever, an event recorded by the parish priest.

Another recent addition is an 1820 inlaid table attributed to Philadelphia furniture maker Anthony Quervelle. According to family lore, the table was used by the Marquis de Lafayette. Restoration continues whenever new information about either the house, the era or the occupants turns up. Recently French visitors brought an 1828 photo of Destrehan that shows the home's original front door. New doors that match the photo are planned. Over the last few years, both the kitchen and a bedroom were altered by furnishing consultant Don Didier to more accurately reflect their use in 1840.

The tour included an array of information about Destrehan's occupants—from a widow who supervised the digging of the Harvey Canal, to a wife who died in an unsolved murder. The guide took great care to explain the history, since last names of family members seemed to change with each generation.

Other aspects of the house's history have yet to be incorporated in the tour. For example the largest slave uprising in the United States began upriver from Destrehan in 1811. Sixty slaves were recorded killed in the fighting. After martial law was declared and the revolt was brought under control, a trial was held at Destrehan. Twenty-one slaves were convicted and executed, their heads displayed on posts between Destrehan and New Orleans.

In a happier vein, the tour notes Destrehan was the scene of a highly successful operation by the Freedman Bureau of Louisiana. An average of 711 freed slaves worked the plantation daily for wages, medical care, clothing, and rations between 1862 and 1866.

NEARBY – ORMOND PLANTATION

Ormond Plantation lies on the other side of the Highway 310 bridge, a short distance upriver from Destrehan Plantation. Built in 1790, two of its many owners died untimely and mysterious deaths. The first disappeared from his dinner table in 1798 and was never seen by his family again. One hundred and one years later another owner was called out of the house at night and brutally murdered. At present, Ormond is a bed and breakfast and private home, though tours are given as well.

UPRIVER – GODCHAUX HOUSE

Godchaux House in Reserve is also slated for restoration by the River Road Historical Society. The house was moved to a new site on the River Road in 1994. A 1909 Godchaux family photo shows President Taft and principals of the Godchaux Sugar Company posing on a double stair, now missing, in front of this house. Though the research was not complete at this writing, the center portion of the Godchaux house is believed to date from 1764, making it the area's oldest house. The historical society plans a museum to house memorabilia from the Godchaux family and Godchaux Sugar Company, including documentation on the early days of the sugar industry in southern Louisiana.

Built in 1790, Ormond Plantation features house tours and a bed and breakfast.

ORMOND PLANTATION

13786 River Road
Destrehan, LA 70047
(504) 764-8544
By admission: $$

GODCHAUX HOUSE

Corner of W. 10th Street and River Road
Reserve, LA
Closed to the public but visible from the road.

Global Wildlife Center

BOARD THE WAGON TRAINS TO VIEW EXOTIC ANIMALS IN THE WILD

HOW TO GO:
Take the Causeway north across Lake Pontchartrain. Follow signs to I-12 west. Exit 47 at Robert on Hwy. 445. Cross Hwy. 190 after two miles, continue north and follow signs to Hwy. 40 east (10 1/2 miles). Global Wildlife Center is on your right.
OR
Take the bus: A new tour service picks up at the Natchez dock behind Jax Brewery in the French Quarter and drops off at downtown New Orleans hotels. Call (800) 543-6362 for times and prices.

BEST TIMES TO GO:
Open seven days a week, 9:00 AM to sunset. Closed Christmas Day. Reservations are recommended. Call for tour times.

GLOBAL WILDLIFE CENTER
(504) 624-WILD
By admission: $$

CAJUN DELIGHT

Two and one-half miles east on Hwy. 40 at Eddie's Food Mart, the Cranky Corner BBQ serves a hearty buffet lunch. A low-price plate lunch includes two vegetables, jambalaya, BBQ pork, hush puppies, bread, and iced tea. Open only Mon. - Fri.

W hen entertaining visitors, I usually choose activities native to Louisiana. So I wondered whether to take a jet-lagged Russian journalist and his Norwegian wife and children to Global Wildlife Center near Folsom, Louisiana. After all, we'd be seeing gazelles and giraffes, not alligators and nutria. Fortunately, Global Wildlife serves a healthy portion of one of Louisiana's real specialties: passing a good time. It also does a fine job of educating people about wild animals.

The hour's drive north went quickly. My friends asked about everything from the length of the causeway to the depth of Lake Pontchartrain. On the north shore, thick woods draped with blooming wisteria eventually gave way to savannah-like fields dotted with herds of unfamiliar hoofed animals. Finally, we were there. On a grassy spot in front of Global Wildlife's administration building, we spread out a picnic lunch and were promptly invaded by a hungry moose.

"We have trouble with moose at home too," said the Russian putting on his shoes and preparing to run. "They come out of the mountains and stand on the railroad tracks. Someone discovered that dried wolf urine would keep them away and sold it to the government. It made them millionaires," he said.

"Where can we get some?" I asked, guarding my smoked salmon as the moose circled our picnic blanket. Then a Global Wildlife employee appeared with a bucket of moose food, patiently luring the towering beast away.

For our tour we bought cups of corn kernels and joined about 75 other visitors climbing onto a train of tractor-drawn wagons. We clutched our corn and the hands of expectant children, as the tractor lurched toward the animal herds over bumps and muddy ruts. Our tour guide explained that we were not to leave our wagons, but were free to stand up and move around when the wagon train stopped.

"Feed the animals with the cup, not your hands," warned the guide as we stopped amid a half dozen of giraffes. We needed to know the rules, but the giraffes and all the other beasts already knew them. Our wagons were quickly surrounded by all kinds of animals, ready and willing to nibble. When the first giraffe stuck his head beneath the wagon's canopy, the savannah rang with delighted laughter. Our guide talked non-stop about species behavior, but was drowned out as excited adults and children alike leaped to their feet to avoid a probing snout.

"This is great!" said the Russian friend, aiming his Nikon at a camel's eye. His daughter giggled, and offered her entire cup of

corn to the first giant zebra she had ever seen.

As our wagon train trundled along we heard about animal "dating" habits, differences between bison and buffalo, and why some animals lose their horns. We learned that Global Wildlife is a non-profit organization whose long-term goal is to

Feeding free roaming giraffes and other exotic creatures is part of the fun at the Global Wildlife Center.

breed enough animals to replenish wild stock. The tour was the perfect length: the littlest kids were tired but the adults still had enough energy to take them home.

As we gathered sleeping children and returned to our cars for the drive home, my friends analyzed the experience in Norwegian, then painstakingly translated:

"It was somehow so human when we were out there because we were in the wagon and the animals were free instead of being in a cage," the Norwegians said. "It's more the way nature should be—the animals shouldn't be prisoners for our pleasure."

DETOUR – ZEMURRAY GARDENS (SPRING ONLY)

It's hard to drag my husband away from New Orleans, but when I finally got him to Zemurray Gardens, fifteen minutes away from Global Wildlife, he acted like the trip had been his idea. He roamed from one azalea-lined path to another, while I sat on a marble bench drawing and daydreaming. Closing my eyes, I listened, and heard only the sound of a thousand bees tending a hundred-and-fifty acres of blooming azaleas.

"ZZZEMURRAY, ZZZEMURRAY, ZZZEMURRAY," said the bees. A powerful fragrance of fresh dirt, azaleas, and pine needles made my head swim. In the cool shadows under the loblolly and slash pines, the azaleas bloom later than most garden varieties. Here a dazzle of Snow White, Peach Blow, and Formosa azaleas formed a solid blooming aisle both in front and behind me. I was beginning to enjoy my solitude, and settled into a peaceful meditation overlooking the 20-acre lake in the garden's center.

"...So this was the playground of Sam 'the Banana Man' Zemurray," I thought. As the story goes, Zemurray only liked practical vegetable gardens and tore out his wife's first attempts at flower gardening each time he returned to the property

ZEMURRAY GARDENS

c/o Bennett and Peters
Route 1, Box 201
Loranger, LA 70446
(504) 878-6731

By admission: $

HOW TO GO:

Take the Causeway north across Lake Pontchartrain. Follow signs to I-12 west. Exit at Robert on Hwy. 445. Cross Hwy. 190 after two miles. Continue north for eight miles and turn left on Hwy. 40. Pass the one-way exit from Zemurray Gardens. The main entrance is one mile from the Hwy. 40 turn.

BEST TIME TO GO:

Zemurray Gardens opens for six weeks when the azaleas are at their peak, usually in March or April.

Hours: 10 AM - 6 PM daily.

Picnic tables outside the parking area by the garden's entrance.

Pea gravel paths are not easy for either wheelchairs or strollers.

DOG LOVERS NOTE

Dogs on leashes are allowed.

"Green things growing are a sacrament," wrote C.J. Stevens, inspired by Zemurray Gardens' 150 acres of azaleas, camellias, and dogwood.

near Hammond, Louisiana. But Mrs. Zemurray and her talented gardener persevered, planting azaleas deep in the woods and waiting three years before showing them to her husband. Possibly thinking the idea was his in the first place, Zemurray took over the project, expanding it to the current acreage and adding statues, gravel paths, benches, and the lake. The result is a property that is lovely all the time, but especially so during the brief azalea season when the current owners open their private paradise to the public.

I guess it proves husbands do come around sometimes. When mine returned from his walk he had a full report: "There's a giant bamboo grove...that's what panda's eat. And pretty white statues all around the lake. Diana the huntress is on that hill. By the way where were you?" he asked.

All Saints Day &
Bayou Lacombe Museum

The north shore town of Lacombe seems to have no center unless you count the smattering of buildings strung along U.S. Highway 190 on Lake Pontchartrain's north shore. The residents, both dead and alive, are scattered like fallen pine needles in the woods between Slidell and Mandeville where roads wind through stands of pine and poplar, linking isolated homes, crossroad stores, and an occasional small cemetery. These roads intersect mysteriously like the Indian paths criss-crossed by animal trails that preceded them.

Life is so decentralized in Lacombe that the sight of twenty or thirty residents gathered around candlelit graves on All Saints Day comes as a bit of a shock. Yet, each year on November 1, the Catholic ritual is played out in not one, but five remote cemeteries.

The ritual begins weeks before, when fresh loads of white sand are delivered to the cemetery gates. Families come to clean and whitewash the graves, spending as much as a day-and-half per grave. They spread clean white sand over the tops and lay out crosses of evergreens. On the eve itself, live flowers are added and hundreds of fresh candles are lit.

I joined in the ritual as dusk thickened into night and a cold damp rose from the ground. Cars pulled to the roadside and families walked the wooded path to the graveyard, following the glow of the candles. Old friends greeted one another, recalling family genealogies with respectfully lowered voices. One old woman who sat quietly staring at graves marked "Ducre" said to her niece, "I'll be layin' right there next to daddy." Young children played hide and seek in the cemetery, unaware of the mystery unfolding around them. Finally, when it was nearly dark, the priest of Sacred Heart Church arrived, gathered his parishioners in prayer and blessed the graves for another year.

The dead of Lacombe, Louisiana are honored by relatives who clean graves, light candles, and await the priest's arrival for the annual Blessing of the Dead on All Saints Day.

CANDLELIT RITUAL LENDS MYSTERY TO RURAL CEMETERIES

WITHIN 1 HOUR

HOW TO GO:
Take the Causeway north across Lake Pontchartrain to Mandeville. Follow signs to U.S.190, driving east until you reach Lacombe. The museum is on St. Mary Street. Turn left off U.S. 190 on 12th Street, go past Joseph Street then bear left on St. Mary.

BEST TIME TO GO:
All Saints Day, November 1, is the day after Halloween. Cemetery blessings are between 3:30 AM and 6:00 PM. Contact Church of the Sacred Heart in Lacombe for a schedule of the cemetery blessings. (504) 882-5229. Wear warm clothes and plan to spend several hours in quiet observation.

I first heard Creole French spoken within the candlelit circle of multi-colored faces gathered around those graves. Descendants of African Americans, French Creoles, Hispanics, and Indians have lived together in Lacombe since the town was first incorporated, and at one time, this area was home to a large population of Choctaw Indians.

To learn more about this unique community, I visited the Bayou Lacombe Museum, located in an old two room school that once served the white children of the area. The museum tells the story of Father Adrien Rouquette, first missionary among the Choctaws. Born to a wealthy New Orleanian family in 1813, Rouquette was educated in Paris. As a young man he traded the New Orleans social whirl for the woods around Lacombe. According to legend, he fell in love with an Indian woman who died of tuberculosis. Eventually Rouquette became a priest and devoted his life to the Choctaws, building small chapels in the woods around Lacombe. There was a vivid description of Rouquette on his death bed at Hotel Dieu in New Orleans surrounded by grim-faced Choctaw warriors. In 1902 when the Federal government saw fit to move the Choctaws to a reservation in Oklahoma, there were 600 Choctaws in Lacombe. The museum contains pictures of Lacombe's last full-blooded Choctaw, as well as palmetto baskets and bead work.

On All Saints Day, hundreds of candles illuminate the pine-sheltered rural cemeteries of Lacombe.

Lacombe's museum also contains information about the area's earliest industries: sawmills, brick-works, and turpentine factories. There are model boats, turn-of-the-century kitchen utensils, old army uniforms, and a piano once played by Louis Armstrong. A collection of newspaper clippings told about the All Saints Day celebration, but shed little light on the origins of the Ducres, Cousins, and Batistes that fill the cemeteries. Bayou Lacombe Museum is open the first Sunday of each month from March through October, or by special appointment.

CEMETERIES:

The easiest cemetery to find is in the curve of U.S. 190, just east of the center of Lacombe. From there follow 7th Street to Main Street, right on Main and park when you see a group of cars. Follow the path into the woods. Osay Cemetery is in the woods across from the Our Lady of Lourdes Shrine on Davis Road. Davis Road intersects with U.S. 190 in the curve. The shrine is on the left, past the the old Huey P. Long Fish Hatchery a couple of miles from U.S. 190.

BAYOU LACOMBE MUSEUM:

P. O. Box 63
Lacombe, LA 70445
(504) 882-5364

Donations accepted.

Bayou Barataria
Fishing Village and Environs

Once a hideaway for pirates, Lafitte, Louisiana, is still a great place to leave your troubles behind. No more than a 45 minute drive from downtown New Orleans, the fishing village on Bayou Barataria features home style country restaurants, historic sites, water views, and a fine bed and breakfast.

The truth is everything about Lafitte feels rural: "town" is a few miles of scattered buildings and boat yards spread along the bayou with a single blinking stoplight marking the center. When I visited bed and breakfast owners, Dale and Roy Ross, my car radio played classical music from New Orleans, but I felt miles from city lights, driving between wooden fences toward Victoria Inn's grassy, lakefront clearing. The new three-story house with an exterior stair and veranda, was built in a raised, Caribbean style by Roy Ross, a contractor from Belize.

"This is how we lived in Belize," Roy said, pointing to the building's wide verandas. The houses are "built up so you can catch the breeze from the water." Then he gestured toward a second Caribbean style home peeking through the trees: "Our house has no air conditioning and we are usually quite cool. Our guests appreciate air conditioning in the bed and breakfast, but we've been here 15 years with fans alone."

Lafitte is often 6 to 10 degrees cooler than New Orleans in the summer—and slightly warmer in the winter.

I explored the town with Dale Ross, a Lafitte native of boat building stock, and learned that people here have little need to look for their roots—they're usually still entwined with them. Families spread out on narrow strips of land stretching between the road and the bayou. Parents often live next to the boat dock or family shipyard on the bayou. Succeeding generations live in trailers or small houses closer to the road. When the family feels it can no longer keep up their road, they turn it over to the parish for maintenance, choosing their own street name in the process. The whimsical results—Lafitte Frozen Food Lane, Shipyard Road,

RETREAT TO A FISHING VILLAGE JUST MINUTES FROM NEW ORLEANS

HOW TO GO:
Take the Westbank Expressway from downtown to Barataria Boulevard (LA 45) turn left. Turn left again on LA 3134 and take it past the blinking light across a high-rise bridge over the Intracoastal Waterway. At the end of the bridge, double back and follow signs for LA 45 again. Drive south with Bayou Barataria on the left 7 1/4 miles to Goose Bayou Bridge. Victoria Inn is on the left just beyond the bridge.

VICTORIA INN
Hwy. 45 Box 545B
Lafitte, LA 70067
(504) 689-4757

SWAMP TOURS:
LIL' CAJUN SWAMP TOURS
(800) 725-3213

LOUISIANA SWAMP TOURS
(504) 689-3599

JEAN LAFITTE SWAMP TOURS
(504) 689-4186

Waterways are just as important as roadways for residents of Lafitte.

13

FISHING CHARTERS:

RIPPS INLAND CHARTERS
(504) 689-2665

BOAT RENTALS:

JOE'S LANDING
(504) 689-7966

RESTAURANTS:

VOLEO'S SEAFOOD
(504) 689-3889

BOUTTE'S
(504) 689-3889

RESTAURANT DES FAMILLES
(504) 689-7834

CANOE RENTALS AND CAJUN FAIS DOS DOS:

BAYOU BARNS
(504) 689-3889

EARL'S BAR
(504) 689-3271

and Willie May Street—are found on green and white street signs up and down the bayou.

Many of the narrow lanes have their own family cemetery plots visible from Highway 45—especially on All Saints Day when flowers and candles mark tombs on both sides of the bayou. One cemetery is built around an Indian mound near the dilapidated remains of the Fleming Plantation, just north of town.

I climbed to the summit of the Indian mound, and under the shade of a spreading live oak looked back at the scores of old tombs spilling down the sides to the bayou's edge. I saw tomb carvings and dates from well before the Civil War, but was most moved by what locals claim is an illegitimate child's grave, set alone and simply marked, "Here lies Oscar...."

Lafitte's locals are no strangers to hardship, especially storms and floods. In 1985, Hurricane Juan smashed boats, tore houses off foundations, and even lifted coffins out of their tombs. "People were out in boats grabbin' Grandma's casket and tying it to the fence so it wouldn't float away," said Dale Ross.

The hazards of flooding and Lafitte's location helped preserve a small town atmosphere. "No need to lock things up—the only thing that's at risk is a small boat and a small engine that might look too tempting to a kid. Little boys get their first boat at nine. It's a safe area. All soft landings here," said Roy Ross.

Nature's seasons dictate the work lives of Lafitte's residents. Most people work at least four jobs: they trawl for shrimp; when that stops, they run catfish; they crab when the crabbing's good; and if nothing else is working, they trap. Ninety percent of Lafitte's residents are fishermen.

The fruits of self-sufficiency were evident everywhere in Lafitte, especially along the levee. Waist-high holding pens fashioned of scrap metal held "buster" crabs, old furniture propped up fishing poles, and homemade ice lockers were ready for storage in the holds of fishing vessels.

The technique for harvesting soft-shell crabs was developed by residents of Lafitte who noticed crabs retreated to the willows when they were

Artist J.P. Scott recycles Lafitte's leftovers into model boats and colorful assemblages that have been displayed in the New Orleans Museum of Art. His yard shrine is visible from Lafitte's main road.

about to shed. They simply hung willows on lines in an area where harvesting was easy and waited.

All the signs of fishing made me hungry. I found delicious oysters at Higgins Seafood, but as visitors to Lafitte's Seafood Festival (the first week in August) can tell you, the area's seafood doesn't end with oysters. All three of Lafitte's restaurants serve tasty versions of the local catch: softshell crab, flounder, shrimp, and even alligator.

Shaded by a live oak atop an Indian mound, Fleming Cemetery overlooks the Intracoastal Canal.

I sampled a flavorful fried shrimp po' boy and spicy alligator soup at Voleo's Seafood Restaurant at the end of the road in Lafitte. Voleo's adds Bavarian menu items to the local fare. Nearby Boutte's sports an upstairs room overlooking the bayou and huge portions of flounder. Restaurant Des Familles, the newest most upscale member of the trio, is conveniently close to one of Bayou Barataria's main attractions, Jean Lafitte State Park.

Residents of Lafitte and New Orleans have been going "up front" or "back of Lafitte" for generations, following the patterns set by Jean Lafitte himself. He was as likely to be seen sipping rum in the French Quarter as burying his booty on the bayou. Still the real treasures of Lafitte aren't buried. I'll be going hunting for great fishing, spring flowers, and fresh oysters again soon.

NEARBY – JEAN LAFITTE NATIONAL HISTORIC PARK

I didn't have time to canoe among the cypress and look for alligators, but it was easy enough to spot them from wooden boardwalks that lace the swamp in Jean Lafitte State Park. Birds darted in the canopy of trees, filling the rural hush with barbarous screeches and strange clacking.

Jean Lafitte's band of pirates once frequented the palmetto ridges in this shady haven. Shards of patterned pottery, blown glass vessels, weapons and the like, fill display cases in the interpretive center, and a film recalls his legend.

Fully accessible boardwalks, abundant wildlife, and a modern interpretive center make the park worth a trip by itself, but it also fits into a weekend sampling of Lafitte's recreational offerings. Rent a canoe at Earl's Bar or Bayou Barns and paddle under the highway into the park for a quiet self-guided swamp tour.

JEAN LAFITTE NATIONAL HISTORICAL PARK BARATARIA UNIT

(504) 589-2330

Open 9 AM - 5 PM daily
Guided canoe treks weekends 8:30 AM
Walking tours 1:15 PM daily
Moonlight canoe treks at sunset during the full moon. No motorized vehicles allowed. Rent a canoe outside the park and paddle in to fish.

HOW TO GO:

Take the Westbank Expressway from downtown to Barataria Boulevard (LA 45) and turn left. Turn left again on LA 3134. Follow signs to Jean Lafitte National Historical Park.

Moonlight Shrimping Tours

CAPTAIN
BLANCHARD'S
MOONLIGHT
SHRIMPING TOURS
PUT YOU IN
FISHERMAN'S BOOTS

HOW TO GO:
Take the Crescent City Connection to I-90. Exit Barataria Boulevard. (Hwy. 45) to Hwy. 3134 (Lafitte La Rose Hwy.) In 4 1/2 miles turn right on Hwy. 301. Lil' Cajun is three miles on the right.

BEST TIMES TO GO:
May 15 - July 1 for brown shrimp season and August 15 - December 20 for white shrimp. Call ahead before leaving the city to check weather conditions.

MOONLIGHT SHRIMPING TOURS & LIL' CAJUN SWAMP TOURS

Box 397A, Isle Bonne Road
Hwy. 301
Lafitte & Barataria
70072
Fee: $$$$
(800) 725-3213

Captain Cyrus Blanchard runs Lil' Cajun swamp tours year-round and Moonlight Shrimping Tours during shrimping season.

I n other places, full moons are associated with romance, were-wolves, and crowded emergency rooms. In Louisiana, generations of shrimpers have caught their aquatic prey by the light of the moon. Now you can don shrimpers' boots, motor down the bayou, and try your hand at harvesting the sea. During white and brown shrimp seasons, Captain Cyrus Blanchard of Lafitte takes groups of four or more for an innovative and educational moonlight shrimping tour.

My touring companions were a family from Asheville, North Carolina, who had taken Blanchard's swamp tour the day before and had come back for more. "Cyrus invited us in and made us feel right at home. Where we come from people are friendly. They want to know who you are, where you're from, and what your kids are doing, so the next time they see you they can ask, 'How was your vacation in New Orleans?'" said Ramona Childers. True to her word Childers told me all about herself by the time we'd donned our shrimpers' boots. She is an operating room nurse who had hoped for a low stress vacation with her husband and kids—and this was just perfect.

Blanchard started the engine and we headed down the bayou with the sunset at our backs. We stopped briefly at an old wooden dock, collecting a basket of ice and shrimp, and a bucket of snapping turtles. The shrimp was our dinner and the turtles were headed for Cyrus' weekly soup pot. Motoring south, we helped clean the shrimp, then watched through the cockpit window as Cyrus boiled a big kettle of water seasoned with oil, salt, and garlic.

Dinner was served on deck at the picking table, a white platform with high sides where we would soon be sorting the evening's catch. We ate standing, the breeze blowing our hair as Blanchard pointed out the sights. "There's Schoolbus Canal—I lived there. It was named for an old schoolbus that somebody lived in. This is Bayou Cutler and that's Bayou St. Denis. Manilla Village, where they used to dry shrimp on platforms, was down that way. I lived on the bayou all my life and I've sure seen some good shrimping. My daughter and I caught 1700 pounds right here in two hours one night," he said.

Blanchard lowered the butterfly nets from their vertical resting position to the water's surface. After that it was quiet for a while. Stars appeared on the horizon, other shrimp boats came and put in their nets, and as the moon rose, we began to look like a flotilla of moon-

lit butterflies resting on the water's surface. In daylight, shrimp are caught near the bottom, but at night they move close to the surface. "They swim up toward the light of the moon. The shrimping's best three days before and three days after a full moon," Blanchard said.

When it was time to raise the net, Blanchard lifted the tail end with a winch, swung it over the picking table and let loose the back rope. A pile of scuttering, flopping silver and pink sea life slid onto the table. Cyrus flipped on a bright light. Our white boots, the spotless decks, and the table glistened white, and the iridescent shrimp eyes sparkled like fireflies. With the patience of a master and deft sure movements, Blanchard showed us what to do. Everything happened fast.

The kids were ecstatic. One used the rake to scoop the pile to the middle so the crabs could come out. Another picked up the keeper crabs—more than five inches—and threw the smaller ones back while talking excitedly. Baby fish of every variety came out of our net. Quickly sorting through the mass, we learned all sorts of fish names and how to tell white shrimp from brown. We hurried so most of the little fish could make it back into the sea unharmed. When the excitement was over we hosed off the deck and examined the small pile of shrimp accumulated in a plastic laundry basket. Blanchard lowered the nets and turned off the lights.

As the evening progressed we raised and lowered the nets half a dozen times, shifting from quiet conversation over radar screens and red lights in the darkened cabin to deft businesslike movements, picking through the catch beneath bright lights. I could see why shrimpers really loved their work, but I could also see why so many could no longer make a living at it.

By the end of the evening we had two-thirds of a laundry basket full of shrimp—about 60 pounds, a few dozen crabs, and one or two large flounder.

The shrimp bring $1.25 a pound, but the shrimp Cyrus bought us for dinner cost $1.70 a pound, the ice was $2.50 a basket, gas for the trip was over $75, and the boat itself costs over $50,000. That's why moonlight shrimping tours cost considerably more than your average swamp tour. But it's a small price to pay for such an unforgettable experience.

The guest crew helps Captain Cyrus lower the nets, preparing for the moonlight shrimp run on Bayou Barataria.

AMERICA'S BEST OYSTERS AT HIGGINS SEAFOOD

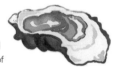

In 1991, the International Food Editors Association had a blind-tasting of American oysters: The Louisiana oyster, *crassostrea virginica*, was ranked best for superior taste and texture. Take home a pint of that Louisiana treasure, right-off-the-dock raw oysters, from Higgins Seafood (504) 689-3577 on Hwy. 45 towards Lafitte. A generous pint runs well below market prices in the city, and Higgins guarantees fresh salty oysters. If you're anxious to enjoy them immediately, lemons and hot sauce are available one block away at the neighborhood Piggly Wiggly.

Pick Your Own Fruit

FRUIT FILLED FIELDS FOR FAMILY FUN

WITHIN 1 HOUR

You may get bitten by mosquitoes, but picking your own strawberries, blackberries, blueberries, and peaches in the Louisiana countryside is well worth the inconvenience. A day in the orchard is fun for the whole family and leaves you with the fixings for pies and jam, too.

Many "you pick" places encourage picnicking, and many sell jam, honey, or picked vegetables. Don't forget hats, sunscreen, and mosquito lotion. The following is a list of places nearby. Call first to make sure enough fruit is available. All places listed here provide containers for picking.

U-PICK-UM: 12088 Marilyn Lane / Pumpkin Center, LA / (504) 294-2393
Grows 17 varieties. Blackberries, blueberries, and raspberries in early June. "My wife just won three blue ribbons at the Hawberry Festival. She shares her recipes," says owner Jim Conarty. Picnickers welcome. Jams, jellies, honey, and picked vegetables for sale. When I called in June, Conarty had just picked 50 pounds of shiitake mushrooms.

HOW TO GO: I-10 to I-55 north to I-12 west. Exit 35 for Baptist and Pumpkin Center. Left 3/4 mile, then left on Tuttle at the U-Pick-Um sign. Half mile and left again on Marilyn Lane. The farm is the first drive on the right.

BEST TIME TO GO: Early June.

B&P FARMS: Route 2, Box 156 AB / Amite, LA 70422 / (504) 748-5554
Peaches, blackberries, and blueberries. Also, picked fruit available for purchase. Picnicking available. Closed on Mondays.

HOW TO GO: I-10 to I-12 west, then I-55 north. Take the Amite exit of I-55, turning right on LA Hwy. 16 for 16 miles through Amite. Left on Dummyline Road for four miles.

BEST TIME TO GO: Blackberries begin mid May. Peach season is early June through July 4. Blueberries begin in June and go through mid July.

FORNEA FARMS: 28392 Louisiana / Angie, LA / (504) 986-2644
Snap beans, peas, butter beans, strawberries, peaches, blueberries, and blackberries. Picked tomatoes, squash, sweet corn, cantaloupe. Picnic facilities available.

HOW TO GO: Causeway north across the lake to LA Hwy. 21 through Bogalusa to Angie. Take LA 1071 three miles. About 1 1/2 hours from New Orleans.

BEST TIME TO GO: Strawberries begin in early April. Peaches and snap beans are in May; peaches, shale beans, and peas are in June; and peas are in July.

Local treasure: These Louisiana strawberries were so flavorful that I ate them all in one sitting as soon as I finished this drawing.

HATHORNE'S IRISH TOWN FARM: Route 1, Box 112A / Amite, LA 70422 / (504) 753-6903

Peaches, blueberries, and blackberries. Hathorne's taped message says, "Bring a picnic lunch. Sit under our 100-year old tree and see our 100-year-old house." Tues. Thurs. Sat. Sun. 8 a.m. - 5 p.m.

How to go: LA Hwy. 43, four and one-half miles north of Montpelier.

Best time to go: June is best, but both peaches and blackberries are often ready in mid May.

M.H. WELLS JR. FARMS: 2025 Weinberger Road / Ponchatoula, LA 70454 / (504) 386-6795 (day) / (504) 386-4502 (night)

Pick your own strawberries. Bell peppers, Irish potatoes, watermelons, sweet potatoes, cucumbers, pepper plants available for sale.

How to go: I-10 west to I-55 north. Exit Ponchatoula and go east to the first stop light. Right on LA 22, and go two stoplights to First Street until it becomes Weinberger Road. At 4 1/2 miles, take a right on Sandy Acres Road. The farm is at the end of the road.

Best time to go: End of May.

PONCHATOULA

There's more than one reason to visit Ponchatoula. Home of the Strawberry Festival and self-proclaimed Antique City, this railroad town has everything from strawberry daiquiris to hand-cranked Victrolas along its main street. The result is a bit commercial, but bargains can be found in Ponchatoula. On most weekends an auction attracts serious collectors from the area, but dozens of antique stores are open almost every day except Monday.

Plan to stop at the Taste of Bavaria bakery/restaurant on the west end of Ponchatoula, then spend the day browsing for old furniture or local arts and crafts. Along with the antiques, there are several new furniture makers in this area, specializing in "Adirondack"-style cypress furniture.

Ponchatoula's strawberry festival is held the second week in April. If you join in the festivities, you won't need to eat another strawberry for at least a year.

HOW TO GO:
I-10 west to I-55 north. Exit 26 to Ponchatoula and go east to enter town.

TASTE OF BAVARIA
14476 Hwy. 22
Ponchatoula, LA 70454
Wed. - Sun. 7 AM - 6 PM
(504) 386-3634
(West one mile from exit 26)

Antique stores fill the main-street of Ponchatoula.

19

Vietnamese Market at Versailles Arms

VIETNAM ON THE BAYOU: IMMIGRANTS KEEP CULTURE AND CUISINE ALIVE WITH PRODUCE MARKET

HOW TO GO:
I-10 east to Hwy. 90 (Chef Menteur Hwy.) Take Chef Alcee Fortier Street, a short distance past the intersection of Chef Menteur and Hwy. 47 or Paris Road. Go left on Alcee Fortier past the stores and cross the bayou. The market is held in a two-story complex on your right.

BEST TIME TO GO:
The market is open only on Saturday mornings. Arrive as early as possible. 6 AM is best.

Most sellers at the Vietnamese Market are older women who speak little English, but vegetable fanciers bridge the language gap with ease.

parked by the crates of live ducks and chickens and followed a crowd of sampan hats into the courtyard of a flat-roofed, sixties style motel building. At 6:30 a.m. it is easy to find the farmers market at Versailles Arms, a Vietnamese community in New Orleans East.

A hundred female Vietnamese voices filled the courtyard, burbling like falling water. At five foot four inches, I was the tallest human in sight. Tiny old women with conical hats and long dresses sat cross-legged on table tops or stood with businesslike expressions next to their displays of produce. Perfectly bundled garden-fresh greens covered each table. Some were tied with bamboo, others washed and carefully knotted into plastic bags. Most still had dew clinging to the leaves.

Very little English was spoken among the older vegetable sellers. But it didn't matter for shopping purposes, since many of the vegetables are grown from Vietnamese seeds and have no English names. Among the greens I could identify were mint, water spinach, lemon grass, Chinese celery, ginger root, dill, and fresh bamboo shoot. I picked up some mint and rubbed it between my fingers. "One dollar," I was quickly informed. Looking further, I learned that most of the packages were priced "one dollar" but little more information was available. If pressed, the women gave cooking directions in broken English or simply smiled and laughed, covering their mouths with their hands.

By 7:00 a.m. the market was crowded with shopping families who greeted each other with happy faces that turned serious for the business of negotiating prices. Everything necessary for a full scale Vietnamese feast was for sale, but cooking the feast required

Live poultry is sold at the market. I saw a family haggle over a live duck, stuff the bird in a paper bag, and drive off in a late model car crammed with eight passengers.

a more accomplished cook than I. Duck eggs were $5.00 a dozen. (Do you scramble or hard-boil them?) Fresh squid filled one barrel, dried shrimp another, and several tables were covered with the stiff forms of whole frozen fish: catfish, redfish, drum, trout, snapper, and anchovies straight from the angler's freezer. Pig intestines, livers, and shredded pork were sold by the bag full. I didn't know how to handle any of these delicacies so I headed for the Asian pears and softball sized mangoes.

Mouth-watering aromas came from indoor markets around the courtyard's perimeter where shop owners conducted a lively business in prepared food. I tasted steamed buns, bamboo-wrapped packages of sweet rice, clear noodles wrapped around pork, and the Vietnamese equivalent of donuts: golden fried spheres rolled in sesame seeds and filled with sweet bean paste. Several vendors vied for the opportunity to sell me a delicious version of Vietnamese "po-boy." Crisp French bread filled with long shredded carrots, cucumber, barbecued pork, and Vietnamese ham capped my Asian breakfast.

Food preparers worked feverishly to keep up with demand. On one wrong turn through a doorway, I discovered a woman making clear noodle wrappers. She had covered two pots of boiling water with cheesecloth stretched tight as a drum. One was covered with a lid. With the back of a spoon she spread a thin layer of white batter on the uncovered cheesecloth, then covered it with the lid from the other pot. She used a bamboo splint to transfer the clear-cooked noodle from the now uncovered pot to a huge pile on the side. Steam rose around her as she worked with a magician's deftness. Our eyes met through the steam, and her perspiring face crinkled with amusement.

Next to a room where "po-boy" sandwiches, pork buns, and eggrolls were sold, I found the source of the market's eggroll skins. An old woman stood over two steaming pots deftly making two skins at a time.

AUTHENTIC VIETNAMESE DINING

If you miss the early morning market at Versailles Arms, you'll still find plenty of Vietnamese culture in the area. Start your explorations with a meal at one of the many traditional restaurants. I recommend Dong Phuong Oriental Restaurant Bakery, 14207 Chef Menteur Hwy., located on the edge of the Versailles Arms community in a cluster of oriental businesses. Be sure to see the bakery counter and leaf through the pages of the sales book of decorator cakes: from Mah Jongg tiles to Ninja Turtles, no special occasion decoration has been missed. Dong Phuong makes an excellent French bread and a variety of Chinese and Vietnamese dishes. On Saturdays and Sundays only, there are hot croissants fresh from the oven. Fresh Gulf seafood is also a specialty. Call first for hours since they are rather erratic in the summer months.

(504) 254-0296

By 8:30 a.m. I was full and had all the vegetables I could carry. I drove through the modern subdivision trying to locate the community gardens. When I found them by walking to the end of a well-worn path through the woods, I had the same sensation I'd had in the market: Could this really be Louisiana? Tightly packed rows of carefully tended vegetables stretched into the misty distance. Several dozen women in sampan hats toiled silently beneath rough hewn pergolas. They couldn't see me and I couldn't find a gate, but as any gardener will tell you, gardening is a private activity anyway.

Back at the market, sellers were packing up by 10 a.m. Families gathered their produce, stuffed their live ducks and chickens into paper bags, and piled into late model cars for the drive home. Everyone looked cheerfully energetic, even the vegetable sellers who picked their produce at dawn. I fought back yawns. Could this be jetlag? I had only driven 45 minutes from town, but found myself on the other side of the world.

San Francisco Plantation

I n 1860 the trip from Reserve to New Orleans entailed a long ride by steamboat and an overnight stay in the city. For the Marmillion family of San Francisco Plantation, and others who lived in great houses upriver, the trip to New Orleans started when they heard the riverboat's first whistle blast and began packing their trunks. A half day later the boat would finally arrive at the plantation's dock, and the family would join cattle, bales of cotton, and other cargo for the trip downriver.

Today, San Francisco is only a 45-minute drive from New Orleans—a monument to nineteenth-century charm hemmed in by the twentieth century. Like a roadside attraction created by a surrealist painter, this wonderful old house displays Easter egg colors and a collage of architectural styles in an incongruous setting, between bulk loading structures and towering gas tanks. A highway runs where the formal gardens once were.

Once past the entrance gate, the highway can be ignored, and the view of the gas tanks is partially screened by foliage. "They are our benefactors," the tour guide said of the neighboring oil company, which saved the house and renovated it at a cost of two million dollars.

A huge bell sat in the garden. Every plantation had one in the days when there were no telephones to spread news among River Road neighbors. Inside, a photograph showed the house as it used to look, with a thousand feet of clipped hedges and walkways creating a foliage frame for a group of young ladies at play.

Touring the house, I could see it was designed for family living. Despite large and formal draperies, the living areas are comfortably small in scale. Every room has a faux marble fireplace and zany, painted wood grain. The parlor ceilings are covered with decorative paintings of the four seasons, flora and fauna. Even the carved Corinthian columns inside the entrance hall are on a human scale, small enough to be attractive rather than forbidding.

Edmond Bozonier Marmillion, the builder, updated the raised creole cottage plan—a common regional vernacular style featuring the living area on the same floor. With architectural details ranging from Gothic windows to Federal stars, this house is a treasure trove for architectural historians. Marmillion's real genius shows in the innovative and practical design elements he introduced in San Francisco. Bricks set into

NINETEENTH-CENTURY CHARM AMIDST TWENTIETH-CENTURY PROGRESS

HOW TO GO:
I-10 to the second La Place exit, Hwy. 3188. South to Airline Hwy. (61) and turn right (east). Left (south) on Hwy. 53 to River Road and turn right. San Francisco is just past the town of Reserve.

BEST TIMES TO GO:
10 AM - 2 PM to avoid tour bus crowds.

SAN FRANCISCO
Drawer AX
Reserve, LA 70084
(504) 535-2341
10 AM - 4 PM daily except major holidays
By admission: $$

French doors, Corinthian columns, signature cisterns, and Easter egg colors characterize San Francisco Plantation

Inside San Francisco, one owner's Bavarian decorating scheme resulted in faux marble fireplaces, faux grained wood, and intricately painted ceilings.

river sand on the first floor keep the lower level cool and allow it to drain easily if the house is flooded. An attic surrounded by louvers lets in breezes off the river and cools the house below. Twelve doors dividing the entrance hall from side parlors are removable making a sweeping, well ventilated ballroom from cozy, cold weather parlors.

Marmillion died in 1856—the year the house was finished—and his 2500-acre sugar plantation, sugar mill, and 17-room plantation house passed to a son, Valsin, and his wife, the former Louise von Seybold. Valsin had met Louise on a trip to Bavaria, and her European influence accounts for the floral Bavarian motifs used throughout the house.

Perhaps Louise was homesick. Between 1860 and 1879 she wrote more than one hundred letters to her mother, and after the deaths of both her husband and her brother-in-law she returned to Germany with her three young daughters, Emma, Corrinne, and

Only 45 minutes from New Orleans, San Francisco Plantation is a nineteenth-century island amid twentieth-century industry.

Amelia. Only Emma married, and much later she told the story of the big house on River Road to her granddaughter, who thought it was a fairy tale.

Louise's letters, passport, and early photos of the plantation home were discovered upon Emma's death, and curious German relatives began to search for the house. Their first efforts led nowhere since they knew the home by its earliest proper name, St. John de Marmillion or by the nickname, St. Frusquin, a derivation of sans fruscins which means "without a penny in my pocket" a reference to Valsin and Louise's expensive decorating projects. Later owners Americanized the name to San Francisco.

In 1981, while attending a conference in New Orleans, Louise's descendants saw a picture of their family home under its mysterious new name. To the German family's surprise, their lost ancestral home still stood, lavishly restored, receiving scores of visitors every day. After visiting San Francisco and discovering hundreds of new American relatives, they returned Louise's letters and photos for the plantation's visitors to enjoy.

Fort Pike

WITHIN 1 HOUR

A jet ski slammed over the waves with a yahoo aboard, zig-zagging across the sea and sky vista which I glimpsed through a gun port at the historic Fort Pike. I could have blown the jet ski out of the water if the cannons hadn't been removed from the nineteenth-century fort. Fortunately, a brisk Gulf wind swept the ramparts, swallowing the whine of its engine and allowing me to trade thoughts of modern mayhem for historic reverie.

As I gazed over the Rigolets—the narrow straight connecting Lake Pontchartrain to the Gulf—I could almost imagine clipper ships passing where the Highway 90 bridge now spans the waters. Begun in 1819 and completed in 1826, Fort Pike still commands the narrows, offering nautical views, cool ocean breezes, and skies filled with scudding clouds.

Fort Pike figured into the Seminole Wars, the Mexican War, and the Civil War. Thirty-foot crumbling walls reveal intricate brickwork beneath, but much of the citadel, arched casements, and exterior walls remain. A one-room museum contains historic photos, mannequins in period costumes, and a model of the fort. There one can study the structure's complex geometric shape, a form based on designs by Vauban, Louis XIV's master engineer. Every angle of the fort was calculated to sweep the Rigolets with maximum firepower. Moats and earthworks camouflaged the fort so that it was not visible until unsuspecting invaders were almost upon it. Even today's visitors may be surprised to learn that there were such extensive fortifications on this tree-shaded point.

Fortified walls and massive ramparts deaden the thunder of cars from a nearby bridge. Few visitors stop by, and the only inhabitants of the fort are the staff of two and several sleepy cats. The fort's core is a citadel used for last-ditch defenses that allowed besieged occupants to fire on all parts of the structure. Surrounding the citadel, open-ended barrel vaults, or casements, lead into the walls, connecting to a damp, sea-level corridor. Here semi-circular patterns in the stone floor trace the path of wheels that swung 30-pound cannons from side to side. Cannon mounts are still visible in some wedge-shaped windows, and each casemate connects adjoining vaults which expelled smoke and eased the flow of men and ammunition.

Impervious in the early nineteenth century, Fort Pike became obsolete with the advent of longer-range cannons during the Civil

HOW TO GO:
I-10 to exit 263. South on Hwy. 433. Right (west) on Hwy. 90 over the Rigolets Bridge. The entrance to the fort is just after the bridge on the left.

BEST TIME TO GO:
Open year round. Organized tours are sporadic.

**FORT PIKE STATE
COMMEMORATIVE AREA**
Route 6, Box 194
New Orleans, LA 70129
(504) 662-5703

By admission: $

Cannon ports at Fort Pike overlook the Rigolets—a narrows through which sailors must pass to reach the Gulf of Mexico.

Eagle watchers have come to the White Kitchen for decades, but a new boardwalk provides a better view of the big raptors that have nested here for more than 80 years.

War. Its obsolescence, however, helped preserve it. For a dozen years prior to the Civil War, the fort was manned by one army sergeant. Confederate forces captured the fort with ease and quietly evacuated when the war turned against them. The result is a nearly intact fort whose linked chambers and solid walls offer shelter from modern life, jet skis and all.

WHITE KITCHEN EAGLE PRESERVE

For years bird watchers climbed the steep back stairs of a telephone switching station on U.S. 90 between the Rigolets and Honey Island Swamp to spy on nesting bald eagles that have returned to the same spot for 70 years.

Eagle watching at the White Kitchen eagle preserve has become so popular that Chevron Corporation and the Nature Conservancy built a 300-foot boardwalk into the swamp from a highway rest stop right at the intersection of U.S. 90 and U.S. 190 providing greater accessibility and a closer view of the still-threatened raptors.

One January morning I gathered binoculars, telephoto lenses, and a bird watching buddy, and went to see for myself. The birds nest in early winter after a summer up north, so this was a good time to visit.

At the isolated rest stop, I was glad I'd taken a friend. The new boardwalk already showed signs of use, and even some abuse, judging by the fresh graffiti. Soon a couple of veteran eagle watchers appeared and helped us spot the birds. One bald eagle bobbed in the nest, while another perched majestically on a nearby tree. Though nearly half a mile away, the birds were so large I could see their brilliant white heads flashing in the sunlight.

HOW TO GO:

45 minutes. Take I-10 east to Slidell. Exit south and then east on U.S. 190 to the intersection of U.S. 90. White Kitchen eagle preserve is east of the Rigolets on U.S. 90.

BEST TIME TO GO:

The birds return to Louisiana in winter to nest.

HONEY ISLAND SWAMP TOURS

DR. WAGNER'S HONEY ISLAND SWAMP TOURS
106 Holly Ridge Drive
Slidell, LA 70461
(504) 641-1769

GATOR SWAMP TOURS
P.O. Box 2082
Slidell, LA 70461
(800) 875-4287

SWAMP MONSTER TOURS
108 Indian Village Road
Slidell, LA 70461
(800) 245-1132

Swamp Tours: The Honey Island Swamp in the Pearl River area is considered one of south Louisiana's prettiest swamps. It's worth visiting despite occasional crowding by tour boats. Most wildlife and flowers are seen in the spring.

Islenos Center of St. Bernard Parish

The Islenos people traded white sand beaches and terraced mountains for the swamps of southeast Louisiana. They are named Islenos after their islands of origin, the Spanish Canaries where they once fished and farmed. Although they arrived amid hurricane and pestilence 200 years ago, the Islenos survived, adapting their farming and fishing skills to the slow moving bayous.

The Islenos Center in St. Bernard, Louisiana pays tribute to the Canary Islanders who settled in the communities of Delacroix Island, Reggio, Yscloskey, and Shell Beach. The center's displays and photos show how they fished and hunted in the bayous, working as a community to weave nets and build boats. They lived first in palmetto huts and then in wooden, shotgun-style houses raised on stilts. The Islenos stayed together over the decades, preserving their own seventeenth-century brand of Spanish—though today, faced with television, automobiles, and encroaching suburban sprawl, the community and its language are threatened.

To get there, I drove through a magnificent aisle of live oaks along St. Bernard Highway. Beyond the white frame house that serves as the Islenos Center, the sight of a soggy palmetto hut framed by dripping Spanish moss transported me to an older time along the bayous.

Inside, park service employee Antonia Gonzales showed early photos of trappers and fishermen and gave directions to the nearby settlements. She assured me that though many traditions have been lost, Spanish-speaking neighbors still gather to build boats, and fish their bayous and bays. Some crafts survive as well. Wooden duck and bird decoy carving is taught at the Islenos Center on Saturday mornings without charge. We looked in the photo album for pictures of the traditional Islenos houses. Since the 1965 Hurricane Betsy, most of the Islenos now live in trailer homes.

While I was there, members of the Marero family came in seeking documentation of their family history in the Islenos Center archives. Other genealogically minded travellers can visit the St. Bernard Catholic cemetery where traditional Islenos names like "Asavedo" and "Estopinal" embellish the crypts.

Keeping Bayou Terre aux Boeufs on my right, I drove south and east in a steady rain,

Stop at any church along St. Bernard Highway and one finds Islenos names like "Asavedo" and "Estopinal" embellishing the tombs in the adjacent cemeteries.

SEVENTEENTH-CENTURY IMMIGRANTS PRESERVE CANARY ISLAND CULTURE AND THE SPANISH LANGUAGE

HOW TO GO:

I-10 to Hwy. 47 (Paris Road) south. Left on Hwy. 46 (St. Bernard Highway) about eight miles. The Islenos Center is on the left.

ISLENOS CENTER

1357 Bayou Road
St Bernard Village, LA
(504) 682-0862

(Operated by the National Park Service in cooperation with St. Bernard Parish.)

Bayou Terre aux Boeufs widens as one approaches the Gulf, and skiffs are replaced by ocean-going trawlers. passing a line of fishing boats that seemed to grow from skiffs to full-size fishing trawlers as I neared the Gulf. On my left, a corresponding row of houses perched on increasingly higher stilts. Beyond the community school, which looked liked a roundhouse on stilts, I joined the stately procession of the Delacroix schoolbus delivering serious looking children to each bayou home. There was nothing between my car and the ever widening canal. The dogs and chickens in driveways gave way to marsh birds and foraging nutria. Suddenly there was water all around. I'd found the End of the World Marina where fishing expeditions begin and driving ends. Retracing my steps I drove toward the two settlements of Reggio and Shell Beach.

Other than marinas and occasional signs for "hog hunts" or "shrimp," I saw no commercial establishments until I arrived at the Food Junction at highways 300 and 46. While I waited in line for one of their sandwiches, I eavesdropped on the local patois and asked for directions to Shell Beach.

At Shell Beach I spotted a cluster of the slender, wooden homes originally built by the Islenos. By now it was raining hard and as the light failed, I saw three or four ocean-going craft leave with crews of men in rain slickers, checking their nets and winches. No wonder those school children looked so serious. In this community of fishermen, many fathers spend nights at sea fishing the Gulf in homemade boats while most of us sit home in comfort. Perhaps the hardy Islenos are not yet ready to surrender to the American melting pot.

Best times to go:

Museum Days
Held at the Islenos Center in March, Museum Days includes boat building, craft demonstrations, and Decimas (sung poetry passed on in an oral tradition).

Good Friday
Three groups of parishioners march to San Pedro Pescador performing Stations of the Cross. They go along LA 300 from Delacroix Island, LA 46 from Yscloskey and Shell Beach, and LA 46 from St. Bernard Village. San Pedro Pescador is at the intersection of LA 46 and LA 300. (504) 676-3719.

Blessing of the Shrimp Fleet
During the last weekend in July and first weekend in August, Delacroix Island and Yscloskey area boats parade and are blessed by the area priest. Sponsored by the church of San Pedro Pescador.

Saint Bernard's Feast Day
Weekend closest to August 20. Islenos Society has a special mass and a tour of the cemetery at St. Bernard Church.

Crabbing the Louisiana Waterways

I stopped alongside Love Road to photograph a fishing trawler and all four members of the Lamparski family left their crab nets and lines to say hello. They appeared to be enjoying themselves on this bright spring afternoon—so much so that I mistook their roadside tasks for a recreational outing rather than the formative stages of a serious family project: making gumbo.

"Nothing else gives a gumbo the flavor but the crab," said Cindy Lamparski as she lowered a crab net back to its place beneath the small bridge on which we stood. "First you buy some crab nets—they're about $1.70 each. Then you get string and some chicken for bait. Put the chicken in the net, weight the net with a little bit of brick and hang the whole thing in the water so it touches bottom. Make sure it touches or the alligator gar will eat out the net bottom." I notice five or six weighted crab nets were spaced out on each side of the bridge railing. Lamparski checked the pots every now and again, which left plenty of time for visiting and enjoying the sunshine.

Lamparski's little boy was employing a different method beyond the bridge. He tied chicken to a string, threw it out a short ways and when a crab approached, yelled for his father who scooped it up with a long-handled net. "We've tried to teach all our kids to crab for making gumbo. We also trap nutria rats, beaver, mink, and fox. If we don't teach them, their kids won't know how," said Cindy Lamparski.

The family gumbo expedition began at 10 a.m. and would probably finish about 3 p.m. A kettle in the back of the Lamparski's truck already held about fifteen crabs, close to their gumbo requirement of "at least two dozen" to make dinner for six with leftovers. I noticed most of their crabs were large and though there is no minimum size requirement for recreational crabbing, the Louisiana Department of Wildlife and Fisheries encourages a self-imposed minimum

Crabbing: The Lamparski family spent a quiet morning filling their gumbo pot on the north shore of Lake Pontchartrain.

CRABS FOR GUMBO: AS FUN TO CATCH AS TO EAT

HOW TO GO:

To try your hand at catching dinner, here are some favorite crabbing spots of locals.

—Hwy. 433 at Salt Bayou.

—Hwy. 434 at Lake Pontchartrain near Lacombe.

—Car Drive or Rats Nest Road - First left and right respectively off Hwy. 11 just north of Lake Pontchartrain in Slidell

—The Rigolets and Fort Pike. Both sides of the Hwy. 90 bridge over the Rigolets.

Inexpensive crab nets are sold at gas stations and convenience stores throughout south Louisiana.

of five inches from point to point. This allows small crabs to grow and reproduce, replenishing the supply. It is illegal to take any female crab with an egg sack attached and it is illegal to detach the egg sack.

Crabbing is a year round daytime activity in Louisiana—nighttime crabbing is illegal. Crabbing is allowed in any of the public recreation areas of the state. No license is required and an individual can possess up to ten ring nets 18 inches in diameter. Crabs should be kept in a ventilated container protected from sunlight or on ice to insure they are alive before boiling. To cook, according to *The New Orleans Cookbook* by Rima and Richard Collins, drop the live crabs into a boiling courtbouillon (water seasoned with crab boil that has boiled for 10 minutes). Bring to a boil again and boil for 15 to 20 minutes, depending on the size of the crabs. Drain thoroughly and allow to cool for 10 minutes.

NOTE: Crab boil is a product commercially available throughout Louisiana.

Laura Plantation

T he plantation house at Laura was built before 1810, but there is nothing old-fashioned about the tour visitors get when they visit this recently reopened River Road plantation.

Laura Plantation's renovation is not complete, and that's how the owners want it. Instead of restoring every room in the furnishings of a single period, they are leaving evidence of the changes the building has undergone during two centuries. Holes in the walls reveal brick-between-post construction and fragments of Civil War cannonballs; sun-faded walls show the outlines of seldom-moved furniture, and pencilled notations reveal the growth of the plantation's children. There are several buildings scheduled for renovation on the property, and plans to incorporate them all into a panorama of nineteenth-century river life. But it is not only the buildings that make the era come alive.

The story of the Creole family that lived at Laura Plantation was written by Laura Locoul (1861-1963) great-grandaughter of the plantation's founder. Her 70-page memoir, hundreds of pages of plantation records, and family treasures from baby teeth to dancing slippers were saved by family and friends, and will be used to illustrate life at Laura Plantation. Life-size cut-out pictures of family members and household slaves are displayed throughout the house. Tour guides know the family characters well and share everything from the inner workings of plantation life to intimate family secrets.

When I visited, St. Charles Parish school children who chose Laura Plantation for a lesson in historic preservation, dressed up in period costume and recited parts of Laura's story. "This plantation was owned and operated by the women of the family," said one small girl dressed in a nineteenth-century christening gown. "After my daughter died, I never left this room," said another.

RESTORATION REVEALS TWO CENTURIES OF CHANGING PLANTATION LIFE

HOW TO GO:

The fast way is to take I-10 west to Hwy. 310 south across the new Mississippi River Bridge to Hwy. 3127. Head toward Donaldsonville and turn right on LA 20, then drive into Vacherie. When you come to the River Road (LA 18) turn right. Laura Plantation is only a few hundred yards on the right. Unfortunately, you miss the whole River Road this way, but to see it right, you need time and good guidance.

BEST TIME TO GO:

The plantation is open year round. It has no electricity, but gentle breezes from the river cool it in the summer the old-fashioned way. A tour at any hour will give you an authentic plantation experience, however a morning visit is best in summer.

LAURA PLANTATION

2247 Highway 18
Vacherie, LA 70090
(504) 265-7690
9 AM - 5 PM
By admission: $
Group rates and private parties available.

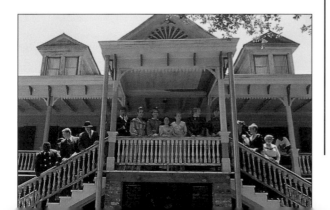

School children get a history lesson at Laura Plantation.

ROBERT'S RIVER ROAD TOURS

One good way to see the upriver areas between New Orleans and Baton Rouge is to take a driving tour with River Road native Noah Robert. In addition to a thorough knowledge of the area's history, he has up-to-date information on everything from current owners of plantation homes to the environmental impact of the chemical industry. French visitors can enjoy a tour in their native tongue. For information call (504) 467-7689 or (504) 647-0305.

Noah Robert of Robert's River Road Tours.

While the stories behind many River Road plantations are remarkable, I was especially struck at the intrigue and depth of feeling in Laura Locoul's recounting of plantation life. I asked manager Norman Marmillion, which story best-illustrated life at the old house. He had to think for a moment because there are so many tales surrounding this plantation, including the Brer Rabbit stories brought from Africa by Senegalese slaves and recorded here by Alcee Fortier.

"This is not as exotic as some stories but it tells a lot about plantation life," he said. "When Laura was thirteen she decided she wanted to leave the plantation. The idea came one day when she was laying on her bed with a girlfriend dreaming about the future. They were both dressed in flapper outfits, and her friend was full of news about a good school in New Orleans. Laura asked her father if she could join her friend at school. He trembled at the thought, and later cried before he granted his permission. You see the plantation passed through the women and Laura knew it was falling on her. Even at thirteen she didn't want the burden. Her father knew that would be the end of the plantation, but he let her go," said Marmillion.

"A story like that shows us the real struggles of life on the plantation. Laura wanted to be liberated from the burdens that women today consider shouldering."

EATING LOCALLY

The Marmillions recommend the Shop Rite gas station on Hwy. 20 near Vacherie for shrimp po' boys and Spuddy's on Hwy. 20 between Hwy. 3127 and the river for plate lunches and po' boys. Spuddy's is also a meat and seafood market.

Oak Alley Plantation

The prime attraction of Oak Alley Plantation is in its name: a double row of 28 live oaks leading from the River Road to the antebellum mansion. Photographers gather daily at the roadside pullout across from the alley, taking their turn with one of Louisiana's most-pictured subjects. Fortunately, the oaks don't seem to mind. They remain rooted in place as they have for the last three hundred years, facing the daily horde of awestruck visitors without turning even one leaf.

An unknown French settler planted the trees at Oak Alley in the 1700s. His house is gone, but he anticipated the trees' longevity, planting them close enough to create a canopy and far enough to keep them from intertwining even now. After the present mansion was built in 1837, one of its early owners chose bankruptcy rather than remove even one of the magnificent oaks that gave the house and plantation its name. Today, the trees are listed as National Historic Landmarks and are carefully protected from lightning and disease. The alley itself is no longer used as an entrance and cars are left in a distant parking lot.

While some visitors tasted Mint Juleps on the veranda, I walked the length of the alley, enjoying its spaciousness and quietness, while imagining life among the cane fields before the era of the automobile.

When the old plantation bell rang, I followed a hoop skirted tour guide into the pale pink antebellum mansion. It was spacious inside—full of the carefully preserved furnishings and paintings of its last owners, Andrew and Josephine Stewart. They were responsible for restoring Oak Alley and opening it to the public. The house clocks were stopped at the hour of Mrs. Stewart's death in 1972.

Near a window overlooking the oaks, an easel displayed the alley covered with four inches of snow. "Mrs. Stewart said that this should not be removed until there is a bigger snowstorm," the guide informed us.

River Road plantations are often used as the setting for movies and weddings. My favorite story about Oak Alley Plantation involves both. When Anne Rice's *Interview with the Vampire* was filmed at Oak Alley, the script called for oaks heavily draped with Spanish moss and a road to the front door. The set designers spent thousands of dollars

A POSTCARD PLANTATION ROOTED IN HISTORY

HOW TO GO:
I-10 to Hwy. 310 south across the Mississippi River to Hwy. 3127. Head toward Donaldsonville and turn right on LA 20, then drive into Vacherie. When you come to the River Road (LA 18) turn left. Oak Alley is three and a half miles upriver on the left.

OAK ALLEY PLANTATION
3645 Louisiana Hwy. 18
Vacherie, LA 70090
(504) 265-2151
By admission: $$
9 am - 5:30 pm
Seven days a week.

Wheelchair access on first floor only, but a video tape of the second floor is provided.

The 28 oaks that form the aisle leading to Oak Plantation were planted 300 years ago and still are perfectly spaced.

Brides love Louisiana plantations. I saw this one at San Francisco Plantation, upriver from New Orleans.

on Spanish moss and festooned the alley, but failed to consult with a wedding party pre-scheduled to use the plantation during filming. When the bride realized how the oaks would appear in her wedding pictures, she put her foot down—and the moss came down too. If Hollywood could pay a fortune to drape those oaks once, they could surely do it again.

Lagniappe – Lutcher and Gramercy – Christmas Eve Bonfires

Fires break out all over St. James Parish on Christmas Eve, but the men of the Gramercy Volunteer Fire Department never worry. In fact, they usually set a few themselves as part of the fiery holiday tradition observed in the small community just upriver from New Orleans.

Beginning at Thanksgiving the 27-man fire department builds an elaborate bonfire structure out of kindling—some say to guide Pere Noel to his Christmas destinations. Each year's creation—from imaginary Everwillow Plantation to a lifesize replica of an F-14 fighter plane—goes up in flames during the Christmas Eve bonfire burnings. But the firemens' duties include more than merely torching the 20-foot structure on the levee across from the fire house.

Every year the Gramercy Volunteer Fire Department plays host to some 50,000 bonfire spectators. They serve homemade jambalaya and gumbo, set off fireworks on the batture, and stand ready to fight unintended fires. "One year a house caught fire in town," said a fire fighter. "We got the call right at 6:45 p.m.—and we're supposed to light the bonfire at 7:00 p.m—with thousands of people waiting by the levee." That year the Gramercy Fire Department put out and started fires simultaneously.

In addition to the fire department's spectacular torching, traditional pyramid-shaped pyres are spaced every 150 feet along a mile of levee between Gramercy and Lutcher where another large bonfire structure has often been constructed. In 1993 Lutcher duplicated Louisiana's Old State Capitol building. Steps representing the 50 states led up to the multi-storied structure allowing visitors to view historical displays inside before the bonfire was lit.

Gramercy Volunteer Fire Department

407 East Jefferson Hwy.
Gramercy, LA 70052
(504) 869-3856

How to go:

River Road is often bumper-to-bumper on Christmas Eve day. Try this alternative route. After taking I-10 or Airline Highway to Hwy. 641, turn right on Hwy. 3125 turn right and then left on Hwy. 3193. To visit the St. James Historical Society and get a spot to view Lutcher's bonfire, park in downtown Lutcher and walk to the levee. The Gramercy Volunteer Fire Department is in a green and white corrugated metal building in Gramercy, one mile downriver from Lutcher.

Best time to go:

Head upriver early afternoon, and be prepared to live with the crowd for several hours. If the wind is cooperating, the fires are set around 7 PM.

Construction of traditional pyramid-shaped pyres begins around Thanksgiving in the river parishes. Crowds flock to the area on Christmas Eve, when hundreds of pyres are lit on the levees.

Chacahoula Bayou Swamp Tour

Jerry Dupre's grandparents acted on show boats, but made their descendants promise to stay out of show business. That hasn't stopped Dupre from donning his coonskin cap and entertaining visitors on his Chacahoula Bayou Swamp Tours in Westwego, just across the Mississippi River from New Orleans. Circling a dozen miles through Bayou Segnette, the smiling pony-tailed Cajun brings his guests whisper-close to nature and paints a vivid picture of Cajun life, while dodging the loud-speakers and oversized boats of other swamp tours.

Dupre is at ease in the swamp and makes guests feel the same. In fact it's a bit like being invited into his back yard. Tours begin at his open air camp on the Westwego Canal.

Made of unpainted wood and built on pilings over a pond, the camp shows Dupre's touch with natural things. He dug the pond where frogs and swamp creatures thrive, feeds the neighborhood's wild cat, and monitors the health of the once-dying cypress trees surrounding his porch. It's hard to believe his property had been a trash dump, squeezed between the businesses that line the canal. Out in the swamp, Dupre ran our flat-bottomed boat onto the bank, checked the terrain, and quietly invited me ashore. In the course of the next two hours, I climbed in and out of the boat many times, learning to recognize armadillo diggings and native plants. Dupre explained that white-tailed deer can run across mud so soft it can't support the weight of a hunter, and he identified egrets by the color of their feet. I saw a bald eagle, an osprey nest, several alligators, an olive green cormorant, two snakes as big as my arm, and a pretty little raccoon blinking in the morning sun. I even learned some French from Dupre who often hosts musical events for Canadian visitors curious about the Cajun dialect.

Dupre has a familiar way with wild animals. He's been known to grab alligators and pull them beside the boat so visitors can touch the skin, dispelling notions of slimy reptilian coatings.

"Once I grabbed a six-foot alligator and he flipped himself over the rail and into the boat. All my passengers jumped up on the seats crying, 'Do something, Capitaine!' So I jumped up on the seat myself. The caiman crawled around the deck

"Eastern Cajuns called alligators caimon *and ones from out west called them* cocodrie," *said Dupre.*

CAJUN SWAMP LIFE AT THE CITY LIMITS

HOW TO GO:
Take the Crescent City Connection to the Westbank Expressway and continue on the elevated portion until it ends. You're now on the lower portion of Hwy. 90. Continue west through Marrero to the town of Westwego. One mile from the "Welcome to Westwego" sign located on the left, turn left onto Louisiana Street and bear right to continue on Louisiana Street. After passing the open air shrimp market on the left, go 1/8 mile. Chacahoula Bayou Swamp Tour is on the right.

BEST TIMES TO GO:
Spring, fall, and summer. Tours are at 9:30 AM and 1:30 PM

CHACAHOULA BAYOU SWAMP TOUR
492 Louisiana Street
Westwego, LA 70094
(504) 436-2640

Chacahoula Swamp Tour guide Jerry Dupre leads two swamp tours a day from his Westwego camp.

SEEKING SEAFOOD?

Seeking seafood? Try the open air shrimp market at Louisiana Street and Hwy. 90. It pays to compare prices between the booths. You'll find some of Louisiana's freshest seafood here: just look for the masts and rigging of shrimp boats on the adjacent bayou.

twice until I grabbed him, wrapped his jaw with a towel, then flipped him onto the bow. Most alligators would jump right over the rail and disappear, but not him. He hissed and growled at us, then turned around and stomped off the boat, as if to say, 'Don't you ever try that again!'"

After the tour, Dupre's friend, Papa Joe, joined us. Dupre said Papa Joe was one of the first Cajuns to give swamp tours. Though now retired in Mississippi, he dropped by to pay his respects to Dupre.

Dupre and his friend were both self-taught naturalists whose fascination with the world around them showed in the stories they traded.

"I saw a squirrel watching cars drive over some hard-shell nuts. After the cars cracked the shells, the squirrels darted into the road to eat the meats," said Papa Joe. Dupre told of changes he'd noticed in local snakes. Lapsing in and out of French, Papa Joe and Dupre complained about the larger tours with their amplified commentary and tall tales of swamp monsters. Pointing at Dupre, Papa Joe summed up a different attitude: "He likes to be the host and he tells the truth. He cannot be a robot in a tour boat."

Angola Prison Rodeo

BRONCS BEHIND BARS: OCTOBER EVENT DRAWS CROWDS FOR COWBOYS AND CRAFTS

UPRIVER 1 to 2 HOURS

HOW TO GO:

I-10 to Baton Rouge. Follow signs to Hwy. 110 north then Hwy. 61 north past St. Francisville to Bains, LA. Turn west on Hwy. 66 and follow it until it deadends at the Louisiana penitentiary.

LOUISIANA STATE PENITENTIARY

Angola, LA 70712
(504) 655-4411

Rodeo by admission: $$

E very Sunday in October the public is invited into the maximum security prision at Angola to see the inmates wrestle steers and ride wild broncs in pursuit of the coveted title, "Best All Around Cowboy." This event is also a chance to buy crafts made by the prisoners, from Western-style belts to decorative wooden furnishings.

When I went to the Angola Rodeo with friends, we drove on the Old Tunica Road, once the only road to the prison, twisting and turning through deep, sandy ravines and tangled undergrowth. This dense wilderness is the last scenery prisoners see before entering "the farm," a complex of fields and security buildings in a bend of the Mississippi River an hour north of Baton Rouge, which houses 4500 convicted criminals, half of whom are serving life sentences.

Just before the prison gates, we joined the modern road to the prison and a mile-long line of cars full of rodeo enthusiasts who had turned out to enjoy the 29th Annual Angola Rodeo. Security guards were everywhere: on horseback, on foot, and in cars. We expected a car search, but instead received a written warning against medication, food, drink, scissors, nail files, clippers, tools, and mace. My friend was turned away at the rodeo entrance because she carried a change of clothing in her purse—a potential disguise for an escaping prisoner.

We were unprepared for the size of the prison. Vast freshly mowed lawns stretched toward the prison farm. Distant fields were dotted with uniform bales of hay. The Mississippi River surrounds three sides of the prison: a barrier so treacherous no walls are needed along its banks. Soon we saw more obvious signs of restraint: double fences topped

Some of Angola Prison Rodeo's custom-designed events result in pandemonium.

with razor wire surround cinder block "dormitories" with armed guards posted in lookout towers.

Cowboy hats outnumbered billed caps in the crowd that milled around the arena hunting for bargains in the craft booths.

Inmate artisans watched the progress of their sales, studying us from a fenced enclosure behind the craft tables. Leaning into the fence, fingers curled around the chain link, they strained to make themselves heard: "That purse for $15, lady!" one inmate called after the guard had quoted $20 for a wallet covered with roses and lattice. The $15 would be credited to the inmate's account for use in the prison canteen. On the rodeo's final Sunday, the best-selling artisans from the previous weekends gather for a second chance at profit. Assistant Warden Gary Frank told me one inmate who sold $1600 by the second week, may make as much as $2500 before the rodeo's end.

To watch the rodeo, go early and find a seat near the chutes where most of the action occurs in Angola's small arena. The gates open at 11 a.m., and the rodeo begins at 2 p.m, allowing visitors plenty of time to enjoy a hard driving prison rock band. Generally the stands fill to capacity. Latecomers are turned away.

Some of Angola's rodeo events—bronc and bull riding, for example—are familiar to rodeo fans. Others are peculiar to Angola. In the Bust Out, six mean looking steers with six riders spin out of the chutes simultaneously in a whirling mess of horns and hoofs and flying inmates.

Unless they are assigned to care for the guards' horses, inmates have little chance to practice rodeo skills, leaving them unprepared for the ups and downs of the rodeo arena. Still, the inmates were ready to try almost anything: they milked wild cows, flipped 500 pound "calves" to the ground, and snatched a poker chip from between the horns of a bull. They suffered black eyes and pulled tendons with a touch of humor. Prison officials who volunteer their weekends throughout October enjoyed themselves too. "If you don't have a sense of humor in this business, you're lost," commented Warden Frank.

NEARBY – THE BLUFFS ON THOMPSON CREEK

Rodeo not your sport? Try The Bluffs—an Arnold Palmer-designed golf course in nearby Jackson, Louisiana. This 18-hole course offers sporting challenges, and great views of the rolling countryside and streams of English Louisiana. The fine clubhouse restaurant is also open to the public.

For a fee ($$$$), non-members can play the course and go home, or stay in the lodge and enjoy pool and grounds.

The golf course designed by Arnold Palmer at The Bluffs is set amid 674 acres of woods overlooking Thompson Creek near Jackson.

THE BLUFFS

6495 Freeland Road
P.O. Box 1220
St. Francisville, LA 70775
(504) 634-3410

HOW TO GO:

Approximately two miles south of St. Francisville, turn east off Hwy. 61 on LA 965. Drive six miles, then turn right on Freeland Road at The Bluffs sales center. The clubhouse is 3/4 mile beyond.

BEST TIME TO GO:

The Bluffs are busy March and April, and again in October and November. Off-season rates for suites in the lodge apply between December and February.

Louisiana State Capitol

TALES OF POLITICAL INTRIGUE AND ASSASSINATION PUNCTUATE TOUR OF HUEY LONG'S OPULENT ART DECO CAPITOL BUILDING

HOW TO GO:

I-10 to Baton Rouge. Hwy 110 N.—right exit on Capitol Access Road. Left at Department of Transportation Bldg. (end of the exit). You will pass the current Governor's Mansion on the right. Take the first left past the mansion and follow the road around. The capitol building is on the right. Turn right into the parking lot. If it's full, continue through the parking lot and take the first left-hand driveway. The capitol building is handicap accessible.

BEST TIME TO GO:

Early morning is least busy.

LOUISIANA STATE CAPITOL CONVENTION AND VISITORS BUREAU

Open seven days.
First floor 8 AM - 4 PM
Observation deck
8 AM - 4:30 PM
(800) LAROUGE

ontroversial during construction, exotic in its infancy and loaded with memories today, the Louisiana State Capitol building in Baton Rouge has attracted visitors since its completion in 1932. Governor Huey Long's 34-story Art Deco tower—still tallest capitol building in the nation—was narrowly approved in a special session of the legislature. The governor himself stood in the back of the chamber and coaxed the last consenting votes. Only three years after this monument to gubernatorial power was completed, Long was gunned down just outside the brass elevator at the back of the first floor. He is buried in front of the capitol beneath a portrait statue surrounded by manicured gardens. Before taking the official capitol building tour, I paused by the statue and noted that Long faced the capitol building rather than the rest of the state.

Pleasant and informative tour guides conduct the 20 minute tour. Accustomed to entertaining crowds of curiosity seekers, they take pains to stand in the exact spot of Long's assassination and point out a pencil embedded in the lofty ceiling of the Senate chamber by a 1970 bomb blast. I was particularly fascinated with that room's acoustical tile which is made from bagasse, a by-product of sugarcane. From my vantage on the hushed Senate floor, I could see that the elaborately stencilled ceiling had held up well since the 1930s despite constant political haranguing and a bomb-driven pencil projectile.

It's fun to pick out some of the building's symbolic details:

—The capitol's shallow steps are carved with the names of the lower

Former governor Huey Long is buried beneath this statue, facing the Art Deco capitol building which he erected in the 1930s. When current governor Edwin Edwards announced his intention not to run for a fifth term, he asked to join Long in perpetuity: "At this point in my life, if you asked me what I would like as the last legacy or the last tribute that the people of this state would give to me it would be to be buried on the Capitol grounds adjacent to or facing [Huey Long's] statue," said Edwards in June 1994.

48 states in the order of their admittance to the Union.

—Squadrons of pelicans, Louisiana's state bird, fly around the building's decorative friezes of carved wood and stone.

—Carved figures representing law, science, philosophy, and art gaze out from a ledge on the 22nd floor.

—Legislators and citizens alike are welcome to review their conscience in the basement Meditation Room where a list of "State Mothers" is on display.

Art Deco images of Louisiana's bird and plant life are carved in wood and stone, cast in bronze, and etched in glass throughout the Louisiana State Capitol.

If you become bored with symbols, you can stick your fingers in the bullet holes in the walls, memorize the faces of the governors of Louisiana, climb to the observation deck on the 27th floor, shop in gift stores, and have breakfast and lunch in the same room as the legislators. State senators and representatives dine in a roped-off area. There's also a fine collection of Louisiana crafts in the basement.

OLD GOVERNOR'S MANSION

Across town, Long also built the Old Governor's Mansion. Now open to the public on weekends, this pillared Georgian home is imposing enough, but seems a little worn and ordinary after the capitol building. Of course, few of its nine resident governors were ordinary. The mansion was home to such legends of Louisiana politics as Earl Long and country-western singer Jimmy Davis.

Back in the '30s, Huey had yearned for a more fitting gubernatorial manse than the frame house he inherited with the job. The legislature didn't see it his way and refused to appropriate funds. In a characteristically forceful move, Long declared the old house termite-ridden and had it torn down overnight by state penitentiary inmates. Naturally the legislature gave in because they couldn't have their governor residing in hotels. The "friend of the little man" spent $172,000 to build and furnish the place in the midst of the Great Depression. It had a ten-car garage, sunken rose garden and its own laundry, all novelties in 1930s Louisiana.

Today the rose garden is a parking lot and many of the original furnishings are gone, but a number of rooms have been restored in period styles and are decorated with evocative memorabilia—from Huey Long's green Chinese silk pajamas to Jimmy Davis' gold record, "You Are My Sunshine." The tour is self-guided and requires some imagination, but I picked up enough trivia to paint a mental picture of several larger-than-life Louisiana politicians.

OLD GOVERNOR'S MANSION

502 North Boulevard
Baton Rouge, LA
For tours or information contact:
Louisiana Arts and Science Center
Sat. 10 AM - 4 PM and Sun. 1 AM - 4 PM
(504) 344-LASC

Admission charged Sat. $
Sunday free

HOW TO GO:
I-10 to Government Street. North or right on St. Charles Avenue. Right on North Street. The building is on the right.

BEST TIMES TO GO:
Weekends only.

LSU Museum of Art
and Hill Memorial Library

HIDDEN TREASURES ON COLLEGE CAMPUS

HOW TO GO:

One hour. I-10 to Baton Rouge. Exit Dalrymple Drive. Follow between the lakes and onto the campus. Stop at the visitor center on the right just past the intersection of Highland Road for a parking pass and directions.

BEST TIME TO GO:

If you can avoid the school year, parking will be easier.

LSU MUSEUM OF ART

(formerly Anglo American Museum)
(504) 388-4003
Weekdays 9 AM - 4 PM
Sat. 10 AM - 12 PM and 1 - 4 PM
Sun. 1 - 4 PM
Free admission.

There is a fee for tours of 20 or more. Arrange in advance.

Interested in American silver? Take a trip to Baton Rouge's LSU Museum of Art which has the nation's largest public collection of New Orleans made silver. The "Kool-Aid" pitcher shape is characteristic of the local style.

The world's largest public collection of New Orleans-made silver resides at the foot of LSU's Memorial Tower in Baton Rouge. The 175-foot bell tower has held the LSU Museum of Art's collection since 1962. For most of that time, museum Director H. Parrot Bacot has been snapping up any nineteenth-century New Orleans-made silver hollow ware or flatware he can find. Given the size of the collections of Newcomb pottery and Anglo-American antiques, it is clear why LSU plans to build a new museum.

I tagged along as Bacot showed members of a book club through the museum's permanent collection. We began on the American side with the Colonial Room and worked our way, object by object, around to the Jacobean Room on the English side. One of my favorites was a handsome portrait of Lord Nelson before he lost his eye. When we reached the New Orleans-made silver, Bacot's information-packed descriptions grew more humorous: "Bread baskets are very rare—but we're pigs and have two of them," he said.

Bacot seems to keep a mental check list of objects he wants for the collection. "We have one of the two existing kettles on stands, and I know where the other one is. The owner's going to give it to us because she's from Mississippi," he said.

We lingered over some of the "hallmarks" of New Orleans-made silver: squirrel finials, vessels shaped like Kool-Aid pitchers, and repousse silver fruit bowls. I could see why serious silver collectors come and spend the day "doing silver" with Bacot who has been known to don white gloves and discuss each piece at length.

HILL MEMORIAL LIBRARY

It's a short walk from the museum across campus to the Hill Memorial Library where changing exhibits fill the first floor gallery and upstairs hallway.

In the rare book collections, I looked for watercolors of the flora of Louisiana by renowned English artist

Margaret Stone. Instead I found tabletop displays of porcelain fish and birds made by Royal Worcester along with cast bronze bird skulls by New Orleans artist Ersy Schwartz. As it turned out, Stone's watercolors are in storage but can be seen by appointment. Group presentations on natural history, ornithology, fine printing, or botanical illustration are available by appointment.

On a tip from the librarian, I crossed the hall to the Louisiana Collection Reading Room. Built into a wooden frame above a side alcove was a Works Progress Administration mural by Knut Heldner showing cotton, rice, and sugarcane production in Louisiana. "Some people make the trip to the library just to see this," said the librarian, "and a few years ago they tried to paint over it."

NEXT STOP — MUSEUM OF NATURAL SCIENCE

Some friendly students told me about another campus attraction, the Museum of Natural Science. There I found life-sized dioramas of the Louisiana landscape filled with mounted birds and mammals. In addition to barrier islands and swamps, there are several out-of-state attractions including the Arizona desert, a Central American rainforest, and the original LSU mascot, Mike the Tiger. When I pushed the button to hear Mike roar, the effect was so real it frightened my friends' dog into an embarassing public act.

Moving on quickly, we saw hundreds of mounted birds and mammals, and latex models of fish, amphibians, and reptiles in glass fronted displays. I learned later that the public collections are just the tip of the iceberg: LSU's research collections are internationally renowned, especially the New World tropics collection.

HILL MEMORIAL LIBRARY
(504) 388-6551
Weekdays 9 AM - 5 PM
Sat. 9 AM - 1 PM
Free admission.

MUSEUM OF NATURAL SCIENCE
(504) 388-2855
Weekdays 8 AM - 4 PM
Sat. 9:30 AM - 2 PM
Free admission.

A goldmine for birders: The internationally renowned research collections at LSU's Museum of Natural Science are an invaluable resource for species identification.

LSU Rural Life Museum

AGRARIAN OASIS OFFERS INSIGHTS INTO EARLY PLANTATION LIFE

UPRIVER 1 to 2 HOURS

HOW TO GO:
1-10 to Baton Rouge. Exit Essen Lane. At the end of the exit ramp turn left, go under the freeway and turn right into the museum entrance.

BEST TIME TO GO:
Spring and fall. Hours: Mon. - Fri. 8:30 AM - 4 PM. Open weekends:
Sat. 9:30 AM - 4 PM, Sun. 1 - 4 PM.

By admission: $

LSU RURAL LIFE MUSEUM
6200 Burden Lane
Baton Rouge, LA
70808
(504) 765-2437

Gardener, sculptor, and founder of the Rural Life Museum, Steele Burden grew up on the property, built the gardens and preserved the buildings and objects that make up the collection.

I entered Louisiana's plantation past near a gas station and freeway exit on the outskirts of Baton Rouge. At that busy twentieth-century corner, a small sign pointed the way to the LSU Rural Life Museum: a gathering of historic buildings and museum displays at the end of a narrow, cane-lined road.

Set on the grounds of the former Burden Plantation, the museum is surrounded by fields of cotton, sugarcane, fruit trees, and a huge rose garden—all part of a modern agricultural research center. Those traditional crops made a perfect backdrop for a long row of antique farm machinery leading to the museum's barn-like display hall.

Inside I found a bewildering array of objects: horse collars made of corn shucks and Spanish moss, a collection of beeswax figurines, a horse-drawn hearse, and glass beaded burial wreaths, called courronnes. Other objects puzzled me so I went to the museum office for assistance. There I met the remarkable 94-year-old man who is the museum's founder, chief benefactor, and collector.

Steele Burden, whose family plantation was deeded to LSU for the Rural Life Museum, sat fashioning clay figures near a window.

"I'm just playing in the mud," Burden laughed. He rose in the time-honored fashion of southern gentlemen and led me to a display case full of clay figurines. Burden has been making and selling the figurines for years and the display case held samples of past designs.

The small clay caricatures were fashioned into tableaus, representing by-gone Louisiana life, from political characters like Huey Long to everyday people Burden remembered from his childhood.

Sculpture is only one of Burden's talents. A longtime employee of Louisiana State University, Burden landscaped the campus. He also put 60 years of work into Windrush, a garden next to the Rural Life Museum. Visitors are invited to wander the paths of this lovely naturalized garden, that features water views, benches, and a collection of European bronzes.

Much of Burden's energy has gone into the collection,

preservation, and display of the hundreds of objects and 24 buildings that make up the Rural Life Museum. Burden's "brainchild" has three areas: a working plantation, a collection of early Louisiana folk architecture, and the main display barn where most of the small objects are kept.

The day I visited, only three or four others roamed the plantation cabins, overseer's house, school house, and sugarhouse, but even a crowd could not fill this outdoor complex.

All the buildings are interesting—especially the dog trot house and Acadian cabin—but I was most moved by the small Baptist church once used by slaves. The ceiling was low, and the benches were hard, yet this was the place slaves spent their precious few free hours.

Back at the museum barn I also examined African artifacts. Such objects help explain the rich cultural mix of a state that owes as much to Africa as Europe.

LSU HILLTOP ARBORETUM

Another peaceful spot in suburban Baton Rouge is the LSU Hilltop Arboretum. Fourteen acres of Louisiana trees and shrubs, deep ravines, and meandering walking paths comprise the arboretum. Try it for a picnic, a meditative moment, or a bite-sized botanical tour. I found a free walking guidebook to plantings and carried it with me down the stair-stepped path into a ravine shaded by arching paw paw and sycamore trees, and leading to a hilltop meadow.

You can almost hear them singing.... A church used by plantation slaves is among dozens of old buildings preserved at the Rural Life Museum.

LSU HILLTOP ARBORETUM
11855 Highland Road
P.O. Box 82608
Baton Rouge, LA 70884
(501) 767 6916
Free admission.

HOW TO GO:
From the LSU Rural Life Museum at Essen Lane travel south to Highland Road. Turn left, east, and go to 11855 Highland Road. Hilltop Arboretum is on the left up a steep driveway.

BEST TIME TO GO:
Open during daylight hours seven days a week.

Old State Capitol

LOUISIANA'S COLORFUL POLITICIANS LIVE ON IN HISTORY CENTER

While painters and woodworkers restored Louisiana's Old State Capitol to nineteenth-century glory, electronic technicians prepared it for the twenty-first. The Baton Rouge landmark reopened in May 1994 as the Center for Political and Governmental History, beginning a new chapter in its 140 year history. Now the soaring Moorish-Gothic arches of its hallways echo with the sounds of high-tech multi-image presentations. Kids watch the face of one governor dissolve into another on an "interactive" computer screen mounted within a picture frame. In Huey Long's old office, the former governor's image appears beside a podium as the text of his speech rolls on a nearby Tele-PrompTer.

Such modern marvels are only one part of the rich trove of Louisiana history accessible through the center. Exhibit subjects range from the Louisiana Purchase to a memorial for Baton Rouge television reporter Brooks Read who left a lifetime collection of photographs and videotaped interviews to the archive.

Sir Walter Scott's romantic tales of castles and chivalry captured the imagination before the Civil War. In Louisiana, one result was architect James Dakin's fanciful design for the state's capitol building.

This living political museum was the brainchild of Bob Courtney, assistant secretary of state. A former television reporter, Courtney saw rooms filled with16mm film that television stations had neither time nor money to use. He had the idea of preserving this material in the state archives, and from there the museum evolved into a media center accessible to the public. Now film researchers can dig into Louisiana's political history via a video retrieval system.

"This facility should appeal to everyone from serious researchers to people interested in general history. We've had lectures on the history of the Louisiana lottery, the life and times of Huey Long, and an academic symposium on the executive branch of government," said Courtney.

The center continues to collect material. A staff film crew has taped many interviews with political figures, such as former governor Jimmy Davis.

"We are looking for any photos, documents, lithographs, maps, political memorabilia, and audio visual material dealing with the history of Louisiana. We are striving for accuracy and fairness as we document all aspects of local government, honoring honest individuals, and putting the colorful characters in context," said chief historian Roger Busbice.

The Old State Capitol is a historic treasure in its own right. Begun in 1847 and finished in 1849, the white crenellated towers overlooking the Mississippi reflected romantic notions found in that era's favored novelist, Walter Scott.

In these halls on the eve of the Civil War, Louisiana made the fateful choice of secession. During the war the building was used as a barracks by Union troops. A fire of mysterious origins gutted the interior, and the Old State Capitol stood as a hollow shell surrounded by jungle until it was restored in 1881. A new entrance, an additional floor, and interior decorating cleaned up the place, but these august surroundings hardly damped the spirit of legislators. Fist fights broke out in the aisles over Louisiana's first lottery (1868-1893) and Huey Long's impeachment trial was scheduled for the Senate chamber in 1929.

Even the romantic design of the old capitol—a collision of cathedral and castle, decked with turrets, gilt arches, and brightly checkered stained glass windows—stirred controversy in the minds of critics.

Mark Twain called it a "monstrosity on the Mississippi."

According to Busbice, Twain associated the building with romantic novelist Walter Scott, an author he despised for encouraging the false sense of chivalry that got the South into the Civil War.

"Dynamite should finish what a charitable fire began," said Twain.

UPRIVER 1 to 2 HOURS

HOW TO GO:

I-10 to Baton Rouge and follow I-110 until it turns into Convention Street. Turn west toward the river, left on River Road and left on North Blvd.

BEST TIME TO GO:

Hours: Mon. through Sat. 10 AM - 4 PM.
Sun. 12 noon - 4 PM. School groups usually visit during the week.

LOUISIANA'S OLD STATE CAPITOL

100 North Boulevard
Baton Rouge, LA 70801
(504) 342-0500

By admission: $

Stained glass windows and gothic arches are featured in the Old State Capitol's rotunda.

LOUISIANA ARTS AND SCIENCE CENTER RIVERSIDE MUSEUM

100 South River Road
Tues. - Fri. 10 AM - 3 PM
Sat. 10 AM - 4 PM
Sun. 1 - 4 PM
By admission: $

A fifth grader suits up for her role in a simulated space voyage at the LASC Challenger Learning Center.

NEARBY – LOUISIANA ARTS AND SCIENCE CENTER RIVERSIDE MUSEUM

Just down the hill from the Old State Capitol, the Louisiana Arts and Science Center Riverside Museum offers educational entertainment with a scientific twist.

You'll recognize the museum by the antique engine and railroad cars displayed outside. Tour the mail car, dining car, and passenger cars, then find the model train set inside the door. A lighted semaphore indicates that the guards are operating the model train, but you don't have to wait for them to find activities for restless hands.

Two areas of the museum, Discovery Depot and Science Station, introduce basic scientific principles to kids of all ages through games and hands-on demonstrations. There's also a walk-in replica of a rock-hewn Egyptian tomb with two human mummies and artifacts on loan from New York's Metropolitan Museum of Art.

On weekends, the museum puts on space shows, sungazing, stargazing, and a changing program of children's workshops. The first Saturday of every month more advanced junior scientists can take a simulated space shuttle trip in the Challenger Learning Center, located on the museum's second floor.

Groups can reserve the learning center for birthday party "mini-missions" on other weekends during the month. Call for details and a schedule of events.

The LASC Riverside Museum is housed in an old Illinois Central Railroad station, whose cavernous waiting areas have been turned into gallery space for the museum's permanent collection and travelling shows. Some of these exhibits are worth a trip to Baton Rouge alone. For two exhibits—Richard Estes silk screens and paintings from Haiti—I travelled to the Riverside museum to see art that was not shown in New Orleans.

Houmas House

oumas House in Burnside is something of a mystery to its owners—and an enigma to anyone who pays for a tour of the house's interior. The tour focuses on the fine nineteenth-century furnishings collected by Houmas House restorer Dr. George Crozat rather than the house and its former occupants, because Crozat's heirs are still trying to find out exactly when the house was built and by whom.

The oldest portion of the house consists of four rooms, two up and two down, connected by an open-air staircase. "Our French visitors think this part looks French, and our Spanish visitors think it looks Spanish," said our guide.

The rest of the house is Greek revival, and as to its origins, the only thing the Crozat family knows for certain is that its builder, General Wade Hampton, came from South Carolina in 1811. When the Greek revival portion of the house was built, the original house was preserved at the rear then later connected by an arched carriageway. No building contracts have survived, and little is known about the various builders or occupants. Even the guide's information about the household furnishings is limited because Dr. Crozat didn't leave any records.

One small but vivid part of Houmas House's story is in the public record. When Union forces threatened to destroy Houmas Plantation during the Civil War, owner John Burnside pointed to his Irish origins, declared his immunity as a British subject, and saved one of River Road's loveliest properties for us to enjoy today.

Like many of Louisiana's historic homes, Houmas House has changed over the decades. The grove of live oaks between the house and the levee are gone, and the belvedere is closed to visitors. Even so, the rural setting lets one envision the plantation as Burnside's wartime guest, journalist William Howard Russell of the London *Times* saw it:

"The view from the belvedere on the roof was one of the most striking of its kind in the world.... If an English agriculturist could see 6,000 acres of the finest land in one field, unbroken by hedge

GREEK REVIVAL HOUSE IS LAST REMNANT OF VAST SUGARCANE PLANTATION

HOW TO GO:
I-10 to LA 44 toward Burnside. Turn right on LA 942, River Road. Houmas House is on the right.

BEST TIME TO GO:
The garden is at its best in spring.

HOUMAS HOUSE
40136 Hwy. 942
Burnside Darrow, LA 70725
(504) 522-2262 (New Orleans)
(504) 473-7841

Between tours, guides at Houmas House relax in the enclosed carriageway that connects the original structure to the Greek revival portion of the house.

or boundary, and covered with the most magnificent crops of tasseling Indian corn and sprouting sugarcane, as level as a billiard table, he would surely doubt his senses. But here is literally such a sight."

Russell, who was sent to report on relations between the North and the South, said it was, "as easy to persuade the owner of such wealth that slavery is indefensible as to have convinced the Norman baron that the Saxon churl who tilled his lands ought to be his equal."

The wealthy owner of Houmas Plantation may have argued in favor of slavery, but Burnside's own humble origins were closer to the Saxon churl than the Norman baron. An immigrant orphan at twelve, he lived out of garbage pails on the docks of New York until he was taken in by a wealthy merchant, treated as a son, and eventually came to manage the merchant's holdings in New Orleans.

Burnside succeeded first as a merchant, building New Orleans' largest house—the Robb Mansion—once the site of Newcomb College. Then he turned his energy toward sugar planting. In 1858 he bought Houmas House and a 12,000 acre sugar plantation, turning the estate into 20,000 acres by his death in 1881. Little remains of this remarkable success story other than his name, which was preserved in the nearby town of Burnside, Louisiana.

When Crozat bought Houmas House from Burnside's heirs in 1940, it had been standing empty for years. He restored the house and behind it built formal gardens modeled after those at Williamsburg, Virginia.

Visitors are welcome to roam the grounds after the tour. Surrounded by off-duty tour guides in antebellum dresses and a pair of symmetrically placed garconnières, one can almost picture Houmas House as Russell described it: "Mr. Burnside and his guests

The formal gardens behind Houmas House are modelled after those at Williamsburg, Virginia, and are flanked by twin garconnières.

sat out in the twilight under the magnolias in the veranda, illuminated by the flashing fire-flies, talking of the war and politics."

CAJUN VILLAGE

Looking for a guide to the profusion of River Road plantations, I stopped at the Ascension Parish Tourist Office and discovered a tourist destination right on the spot.

The tourist office is set among a collection of restored plantation buildings housing shops and galleries known as Cajun Village. Behind the buildings there's an exhibit of live alligators in a natural setting. Located at exit 182 off of I-10, Cajun Village is also a good stop for weary travelers seeking coffee and beignets. It's the only place I've found beignets—a creole style donut —outside of New Orleans.

Cajun Village started as an overflow lot for Al Robert's growing collection of salvaged antebellum structures. Robert owns the nearby Cabin Restaurant and made a hobby of saving and restoring old plantation buildings on that property. Eventually he ran out of room and bought the land at the intersection of Highway 22 and Highway 70. That's when self-taught sculptor Craig Black and his wife Linda, caretakers of nearby Houmas House, came into the picture.

Robert offered the Blacks a year of free studio and gallery space if they would restore one of the buildings. They did better than that, forming Southern Tangent, an art gallery that shows the work of more than 150 Louisiana self-taught artists: painters, potters, quilters, sculptors, and even musical instrument-makers.

Live alligators, crafts, coffee, beignets, and local directions are all available at Cajun Village, off I-10 near the Sunshine Bridge.

CAJUN VILLAGE

Ascension Parish Tourist Center
9 AM - 5 PM
Seven days
(504) 675-6550

The Coffee House
6 AM - 9 PM
Seven days
(504) 675-8068

Southern Tangent Gallery
10 AM to at least 5 PM
(504) 675-6815
(800) 460-6815

HOW TO GO:
I-10 west to exit 182 or Hwy. 22 (the second exit for Sorrento). Follow signs one block to the turn for Sunshine Bridge at Hwy. 70. Cajun Village is at the intersection of Hwy. 22 and Hwy. 70.

BEST TIMES TO GO:
Cajun Village is a great halfway coffee stop between Baton Rouge and New Orleans.

51

River Road African-American Museum and Gallery

RECALLING MORE THAN SLAVERY, MUSEUM CELEBRATES LOCAL HEROES

HOW TO GO:
I-10 west towards Baton Rouge. Exit 179 on LA 44 south. 5 1/2 miles toward the river, Tezcuco is on the left, one mile north of the Sunshine Bridge on LA 44.

BEST TIMES TO GO:
River Road African-American Museum:
Wed. through Sun. 1 - 5 PM
For guided tours phone
(504) 644-7955

Tezcuco Plantation Home Hours:
9 AM - 5 PM daily
(504) 562-3929

RIVER ROAD AFRICAN-AMERICAN MUSEUM AND GALLERY AT TEZCUCO PLANTATION HOME
3138 Hwy. 44
Darrow, LA 70725

Donations accepted.

River Road African-American Museum depicts the history and living culture of African-Americans —many from rural Louisiana.

What people don't understand is that the crux of all the problems—the drugs, the illegitimacy and the violence—is right here," said museum co-founder Darryl Hambrick.

The modest board-lined room where he spoke houses the River Road African-American Museum and Gallery at Tezcuco Plantation Home near Burnside, Louisiana.

"Are some of these people your ancestors?" read the sign above a list of slaves once held on the Donaldson-Clark and Ashland plantations. Some on the list had only one name, and some had descriptions like "maimed" or "deranged." The list came from old county records.

"It seems like people around here don't want to look at their past yet. But we want them to see that through all of the struggles, we survived. There were some good things that came out of that: We were together as a people, had strong family values and developed skills. We built all this," said Hambrick, referring to the River Road plantations.

The new museum is attached to the antique store at Tezcuco. Visitors can view museum displays during store hours. Volunteer guides are available afternoons or by appointment.

Hambrick, a Louisianian who has spent much of his life in Los Angeles, moved back to the river parishes two years ago to take over the family business—one of two black funeral homes in nearby Gonzales. His sister, Kathe, moved here at the same time bringing business expertise and the idea for the museum. They drew on a collection of African-American memorabilia gathered by another brother, establishing the museum at Tezcuco because the plantation's owners were the first to embrace the idea. Kathe obtained a small start-up grant from the Louisiana Department of Culture, Recreation, and Tourism, but donations make up the rest of the budget.

Our talk was interrupted by a Canadian school teacher who quizzed Hambrick on slavery. "We weren't told the whole story on any of the other plantations," she said.

But this museum deals with more than slavery, embracing the scope of African-American experience in this country. I looked with interest at a section dedicated to self-taught engineer, inventor, and musician Leonard Julien who came from the area. There were pictures of Julien with the sugar planting machine he'd invented.

A master brick layer, a self-taught artist, and the first child to attend an integrated school, were among other successful area residents featured in the museum. There were sections on the Buffalo soldiers, African-American dolls, and jazz greats as well.

"We're hoping people will bring us objects and memorabilia from their families. Our future plans include video recordings of some of the elders telling about life here," said Hambrick.

I noticed several tourists walk into the room, look around, and leave again. "Lots of people really don't want to look. It's kind of like returning to a prison you've been to," Hambrick said. "I'm here by choice and they (the slaves) had no choice, but I think they'd be glad to know we're here."

TEZCUCO PLANTATION HOUSE

I left the museum and joined other tourists wandering through Tezcuco's oak-shaded grounds. I found a detached chapel, blacksmith shop, doll house, a collection of Civil War memorabilia, a restaurant, and old slave cabins that have been converted to modern bed and breakfast rooms. It felt like a busy plantation theme park built around the 1855 raised cottage that was the main house. It would be a grand house in most modern neighborhoods, but seemed diminutive when compared to such neighbors as Houmas House, just 2 1/2 miles upriver. Still its 15 1/2 foot ceilings, elaborate ceiling medallions, and period furniture are impressive. The tour focused mainly on the lifestyle of the planter's family. Little remained inside the cabins or the house that spoke directly of slavery.

It was built by Benjamin Tureaud for his wife Aglae, one of the daughters of the Beringer family. There were six other grand plantation homes owned by Beringer along the river: Union, Bocage, Ashland, Whitehall, L'Hermitage, and Bagatelle. Three of them, Bocage, L'Hermitage, and Ashland, can be seen from the road by driving north on River Road 11 miles past Houmas House.

DINING

You can find either a quick meal or a leisurely dining experience in the neighborhood of both Houmas House and Tezcuco.

THE CABIN RESTAURANT

P.O. Box 85 / Burnside, LA 70738
(504) 473-3007

The **Cabin Restaurant** is owned by Al Robert, the same man who brings you coffee and beignets at Cajun Village. Robert fused a number of old slave cabins together at the intersection of Hwy. 44 and Hwy. 22 to make a folksy restaurant that specializes in Cajun food.

LAFITTE'S LANDING

P.O. Box 1128 / Donaldsonville, LA 70346
(504) 473-1232

For elegant lunches and memorable dinners try **Lafitte's Landing**, at the base of the Sunshine Bridge across the river. Located in an old plantation house that once housed the successor (some say son) to pirate Jean Lafitte, Chef John Folse's Creole and Cajun meals are on par with New Orleans' cuisine.

TEZCUCO PLANTATION HOUSE

3138 Hwy. 44 River Road
at Sunshine Bridge
Darrow, LA 70725
(504) 562-3929

St. Michael's Church and Lourdes Grotto

F olk artists often use common materials in uncommon ways, but the St. Michael Lourdes Grotto made of clamshells and bagasse clinkers, a by-product of sugarcane production, is a tribute to the ingenuity and recycling ethic of Convent, Louisiana's early residents.

Guarded by a militant statue of the archangel, St. Michael's red brick Gothic and Romanesque exterior gives little clue to the hand-fashioned grotto within. The traffic along River Road is noisy these days, but St. Michael's interior remains as hushed and serene as it was in 1900. Dim shafts of light illuminate the darkened varnish of mysterious oil paintings and Munich art glass windows shimmer with the images of St. Joseph, St. Augustine, and St. Philomena. Fog horns from riverboats reverberate in the cavernous interior, echoing among mammoth cypress columns and stone floors.

The Lourdes grotto is hidden behind an elaborately carved altar brought from the Paris World's Fair of 1868. Ensconced in its own devotional chapel, the grotto's lumpy "boulders" and shell-encrusted altar look crude in comparison to the handcarved confessionals and fancy metal candlesticks of the main church. Still hundreds of hours of labor were devoted to the chapel, and the painstaking effort shows.

St. Michael's Church on the River Road in Convent is filled with old oil paintings, elaborate wood carvings, and statues of saints, but its most unusual feature is a handmade Lourdes Grotto behind the altar.

Two parishioners of St. Michael's Church built the grotto in 1876. It's a faithful replica of Lourdes Grotto in Massabielle, France, built to commemorate Bernadette Soubiroux's visions of Mary that occurred there in 1858. The builders used an inverted sugar kettle as a mold for the grotto's domed roof. They cemented the large boulder-shaped clinkers in place and added a wooden altar covered with hundreds of small clamshells, each affixed with a single nail. A painted woodland scene and large devotional statues of Mary and St. Bernadette add the final touches.

The grotto proved to be a popular spot for intercessory prayers. Over a hundred marble tablets carved with thanks in

French and English are propped around the base of the clamshell altar. One written in French and dated only four months after the grotto's dedication in 1876 was given by the grateful relatives of Vasseur Weber, found safely after being lost for four days.

With its potent mix of history and folk-art treasure the Lourdes Grotto is an unusual addition to any upriver drive.

PERIQUE TOBACCO IN ST. JAMES PARISH

Perique tobacco—the rarest tobacco in the world—is grown in a sandy spot only 40 miles upriver from New Orleans. The first growers were native Americans who prized the tobacco for its exceptionally pungent flavor and aroma. The seeds were passed to French settlers, and the tobacco was named for a Frenchman who cultivated the plants for his own smoking pleasure. As it's fame grew, "Pierre's tobacco" became Perique.

I saw Perique first at Poche's tobacco shed in Convent, Louisiana. Five women in tobacco-stained dresses sat on a platform at the end of a long shed full of wooden tobacco barrels. With fingers flying they stripped piles of leathery leaves to the drone of television soap opera. The protective silver tape on their fingers and the TV propped up on a tobacco barrel were modern touches, but in every other way the scene was the same as it was 100 years ago when the great-grandfathers of the current tobacco growers delivered their product to the broker.

Later Poche's owner showed me a Perique Tobacco display he built for the St. James Historical Society's Cultural and Heritage Center in Lutcher. Visitors interested in Perique Tobacco growing and other parish industries can visit the museum year round.

Once this area supported several brokers and 40 or 50 families brought Perique to Poche's. I found one of the last Perique growers, 75-year-old Pershing Martin, resting in the shade outside his house near Grand Point. Beyond the tidy garden surrounding the Martin house were cows and a big shed used to dry, process, and store the tobacco leaves. He was a small, lithe man with a deep tan, beautiful white teeth, and a quick smile. I asked him why he persisted with the traditional crop, and he quipped: "You know what they say about a tobacco farmer don't you? He's got a strong back and a weak mind."

Each tobacco leaf is handled dozens of times before it's squeezed into a barrel with a screw jack and aged like fine wine.

Reverent recycling: An upside-down sugar kettle was used to mold bagasse clinkers—lumps of sugarcane byproduct—into St. Michael's Lourdes grotto. The altar is covered with clam shells.

LOOKING FOR PERIQUE AND THE PAST?

See a complete blacksmith's shop, an 800 year old cypress tree and ride a velocipede—one man railroad vehicle—at the St. James Cultural and Heritage Center. Displays on Perique Tobacco, the logging industry, and railroads fill several small buildings on the grounds of this attractive museum. Travellers seeking information about area plantation homes and modern day industries will find it here too. The museum also serves as the St. James Parish Tourist information center.

ST. JAMES HISTORICAL SOCIETY CULTURAL AND HERITAGE CENTER
1988 LA 44
Lutcher, LA 70071
(504) 869-9752
Mon. - Fri. 8 AM - 4 PM

HOW TO GO:
Take I-10 west toward Baton Rouge. Exit Hwy. 641 south to LA 3125. Right on LA 3125 to LA 3193, Lutcher Avenue. Left on LA 3193. The center is on the left at the intersection of LA 44 (River Road) and LA 3193.

The cycle begins in January with a thimble of microscopic seeds which when mixed with ash yields a twenty foot by four foot hot bed full of plants. In April they are transplanted, then cultivated, fertilized, thinned, and trimmed until June when the mature leaf turns yellowish—"like the skin of an alligator," Martin said.

"Then during an afternoon at 3:30 p.m. when it is not promising rain, we cut the stalks with a cane knife and leave it all night until the next morning, when it's limp like a dishrag so we can handle it," said Martin. From there the tobacco stalks are hung in the barn until dry. Then the leaves can be stripped off and pounded. After beating, the leaves are moistened and hand-stemmed by local workers, who are paid by the pound.

A little Perique tobacco goes a long way: only a small amount need be added to Kentucky tobacco to produce a very distinctive aroma. Martin, who does not use tobacco said, "My daddy chewed it, smoked it in a pipe, and sometimes rolled it into a cigarette. There wasn't a mosquito around for 50 feet.... There's something special about the tobacco dust (from pounding the leaves). Put it in a chicken house or on a dog and you will never get lice or fleas. People around here know that and come from miles around to get it when we're harvesting," said Martin.

Neither a smoker nor a chewer, Pershing Martin, has grown Perique tobacco his whole life.

Despite Perique's long history, the story may end in our time. Although it is still prized for blending with other pipe tobaccos and brings a good price, young people in the area aren't interested in growing it. "They all have good jobs in air-conditioned buildings. I don't," said Martin, fanning himself.

Madewood Plantation

Smoke from torched cane fields mingled with evening shadows as I drove along the River Road toward Madewood Plantation in Napoleonville.

All day I'd been dodging fallen cane on the roads and squeezing past heavily loaded cane trucks—so Madewood Plantation was a welcome, if slightly unbelievable, sight. From the road, it looked like a film set from "Gone with the Wind": a nineteenth-century idea of a Greek temple with a white colonnade, wide gallery, and a sweep of green lawn in the foreground.

But Madewood Plantation, facing Bayou Lafourche 16 miles from River Road, is no moviemaker's false front. Overnight guests and visitors on the daily tours are welcomed to a family home that happens to be a National Historic Landmark. Madewood is real in every detail: from the curving egg and dart patterns carved into the classical capitals of the exterior, to hand-painted wood and marble graining that covers doors, fireplaces, and even doorknobs inside the house. The scale of the rooms encourages lengthy steps and a more gracious pace—perhaps an unconscious reaction to rooms of perfect proportion. Twelve-foot ceilings and hallways as big as some houses give the impression of generous elbow room, but not pretentiousness.

Now that every four poster bed is filled with guests and the halls ring with conversation, it's difficult to believe that for a decade the house stood unsold with a $70,000 price tag. A New Orleans family bought Madewood in 1964, and together with a small army of loyal friends, spent years restoring the mansion, simultaneously creating a bed and breakfast and a twentieth-century family seat. Similar stories are told up and down the River Road where Louisiana history—both good and bad—is preserved in handsome antebellum homes.

It's easy to feel like a family guest amidst the heirlooms, portraits, memorabilia, and favorite art works that fill the classical revival mansion. My tour included stops at a painting of Madewood's long time cook and a peek at childhood photos of the current owners as king and queen of a Children's Carnival Ball.

A fire engine could park in Madewood's ballroom, yet the room's subtle colors, elaborate ceiling medallions, and chandelier made it feel intimate and feminine. It's hard to imagine the days before restoration when the walls were so dirty they needed pressure washing.

HISTORY FOR A NIGHT: AN ELEGANT BED-AND-BREAKFAST IN A PLANTATION HOME

HOW TO GO: I-10 to exit 182. Cross Sunshine Bridge. Follow Bayou Plantation signs to Hwy. 70, Spur 70 and Hwy. 308. South on 308, along Bayou Lafourche, Madewood is two miles beyond Napoleonville. Approximately 1 1/2 hours from New Orleans.

It took eight years to cut the cypress, make 600,000 bricks, and build Madewood Plantation House.

MADEWOOD

4250 Hwy. 308
Napoleonville, LA 70390
(800) 375-7151
(504) 369-7151
Tours by admission: $

STAYING AT MADEWOOD

The bed and breakfast rate compares to a top quality hotel. It includes wine and cheese, candlelight dinner, a full planta-tion breakfast, and a tour of the house. There are bed and breakfast rooms in the main house, and there are additional rooms in a raised Creole cottage called Charlet House and a private cabin.

Those who stay in bed and breakfast rooms on the second floor can see Madewood's magnificent hand-carved columns at close range.

A MADEWOOD HOLIDAY

The Christmas Heritage Celebration includes hot wassail, caroling, dinner, and selections from Handel's *Messiah*. Cost is $50 per person. Held the first Saturday in December. Call for informa-tion.

"We were wet all the time and we had one room to stay in with one available bathroom. A dozen friends slept dormitory style in this room, bursting into uncontrollable giggles when people started snoring," said current owner Keith Marshall.

Such nights must be good training for a host. Madewood offers today's visitor a mix of history, twentieth-century comfort, and personal warmth that virtually defines Louisiana hospitality.

NEARBY — ASSUMPTION CHURCH IN PLATTENVILLE

If cemetery sleuthing intrigues you, drive up the bayou to Plattenville, seven miles north of Madewood Plantation, where the 200-year old graveyard of Assumption Catholic Church offers a glimpse into the history of the French Acadians and Spanish Canary Islanders who settled this area. Wandering amid the raised tombs, I discovered the final resting place of Pierre Charlet, soldier of Napoleon and native of Grenoble, France, whose house is now used for bed and breakfast rooms at Madewood. Another tomb inscription—this one in French—mentioned the unsolved murder of Monsieur Platen, for whom the town is named. Nearby I found three identical iron tombs lying side-by-side—a silent testimony to an epidemic of yellow fever in 1851.

The adjacent church has simple lines, but its handmade bricks and old clock tower deserve a second look. The present structure was built in 1856, but the church altar was modernized after heavy damage from Hurricane Betsy in 1965. Stained glass windows, lobed columns, and elaborate Gothic chan-deliers and candelabra survive from the nineteenth century.

Just inside the church doors, a glass sarcophagus holds a life-size, life-like, wax image of St. Faustine, a young girl who became a saint when she was beheaded. Though Faustine has not been included in the church's list of saints since 1960, she remains the parish's special devotion and is believed to be responsible for several miracles. Her feast day is celebrated on April 18 with a procession.

French and Spanish names fill the rolls of Assumption Catholic Church in Plattenville, built in 1856 on the site of an older eigh-teenth century church.

Parlange Plantation on False River

Before the Civil War, before the Louisiana Purchase or the American Declaration of Independence, ancestors of the Parlange family lived near New Roads, Louisiana in the same plantation home in which their descendants still extend hospitality to history-minded visitors.

Parlange Plantation is situated on False River, a picturesque oxbow, festooned with sailboats and ringed with vacation rentals. A pair of octagonal pigeonniers flank the drive leading to the raised Creole-style house. Surrounded by live oaks and a host of kitchen and utility buildings, this mid-eighteenth-century treasure is also a working farm.

Dogs barked and bright blue lizards scurried when Lucy Parlange, the plantation's current mistress, threw open a French door in the kitchen wing to greet me. She ushered me through a dining room where the table was set for twenty, and every other surface seemed covered with china and silver. I noticed carved cypress moldings and fireplace mantles. Cypress floors showed the gentle wear of two centuries. We settled in a receiving salon at the front of the house amid stacked books, old porcelain, and a gallery of family portraits.

"Weekends our house is always full," Miss Lucy said. "Our three children come with their friends...and then there are our friends.... My husband says we should change the name of the house to 'Constant Company'." Though visitors can tour by appointment only, everyone is welcomed into this house as if they are old friends.

Moments later our talk was interrupted by the cries of small children who visit Miss Lucy most afternoons to play. A bedroom that once housed both Union and Confederate generals is now a playroom piled high with antique toys. With Miss Lucy's encouragement, the children played at our feet, while she wandered from portrait to portrait, telling stories of the women who lived in the house before her.

A floor-to-ceiling oil painting of Madame Virginie de Ternant Parlange dominates the central salon, accompanied by three sepa-

ORIGINAL FAMILY INHABITS EIGHTEENTH-CENTURY CREOLE HOUSE

HOW TO GO:
About 2 1/2 hours. I-10 to Baton Rouge, then west on 190 to Hwy. 1. North on Hwy. 1. Parlange is just past the intersection of Hwy. 1 and Hwy. 78.

PARLANGE PLANTATION ON FALSE RIVER
New Roads, LA 70760
(504) 638-8410
By admission: $$
Call in advance for an appointment.

Parlange Plantation began with a land grant from the French king and is still operated as a farm by the original family.

rate oval portraits of her children. This Civil War era hostess saved her home by preparing fine dinners for the occupying Union troops.

The most famous family portrait never came to Parlange. A granddaughter of the Civil War hostess had her portrait painted by John Singer Sargent in 1883. When the picture was unveiled in Paris, it triggered a scandal of international proportions. The family rejected the painting. The full-length figure in a low evening gown with one strap off the shoulder was too provocative for the time. Though Sargent painted a new strap on his subject's shoulder, he was forced to move his portrait painting business from Paris to London. The painting was subsequently sold to the Metropolitan Museum of Art under the name of "Madame X" where it hangs as the centerpiece of the American wing today.

The grounds of Parlange are as artful as its interiors. Once fronted by a formal French garden that stretched to the river, Parlange's landscaping was redesigned with the help of Steele Burden, founder of the Rural Life Museum in Baton Rouge. Now the paths wind lazily under live oaks. Groves of bamboo and carpets of monkey grass provide foliage backdrops for a collection of small sculptures that includes a bucking bronco by Frederic Remington.

The property is full of surprises. One of the pigeonniers is now a two-story guest cottage lined with books instead of roosting birds.

A museum in the basement of the main house contains antique plantation tools, sugar kettles, and the triangular molds used to make bricks for the house's columns.

Triangular brick molds were used to make the tapering columns of Parlange, a raised plantation home built in the eighteenth century.

New Roads Area

The sleepy little town of New Roads at the north end of False River is only a ferry crossing away from St. Francisville, but it might as well be on the other side of the world. While St. Francisville is English, Protestant, and highly-touted as a tourist destination, New Roads is French, Catholic, and relatively undiscovered.

False River has long been a favorite of bass fishermen and there are numerous waterfront "camps" for rent by the week. For more pampered accommodations, New Roads has several bed and breakfasts. A relaxed stay of more than one day will give you time to shop at the numerous antique stores, hike a ten-mile trail along the lake, visit historic Parlange Plantation, and try the locals' favorite eatery, Joe's "Dreyfus Store" Restaurant in Livonia.

I visited New Roads in December and began my shopping at Ol' Man River Antiques, where I found first editions, a variety of inexpensive teapots and antique cooking utensils. The cooks on my Christmas list also benefitted from my next stop: the Bergeron Pecan Shelling Plant just south of New Roads. Southern pecans are a gift appreciated in parts of the country where nut prices never fluctuate with the harvest and fresh products are hard to find. You can visit the factory from October through April.

At Bergeron's I found small local pecans, called "natives," and a few large fancy ones at prices well below any I've seen in city grocery stores.

One of only two "cracking" houses in Louisiana, Bergeron sometimes operates seven days a week to keep up with the demand. But Lester Bergeron, grandson of the company's founder, didn't seem to mind interrupting his hectic schedule to give tours.

The factory and everyone in it was covered with a fine red powder and a warm, brown, nutty smell filled the air. It was too loud to talk in the factory, so we walked between barrels full of unshelled pecans looking at the complicated machines for washing, cracking, hulling, and sorting nuts. Some of the machines looked like elaborate gambling games, with pecans tumbling through slots and chutes. Others jiggled madly, sorting nuts through mesh screens. At the end of the line three women sat side-by-side scrutinizing the sized nut halves for misfits.

"When my grandfather started the business, local sharecroppers took nuts home to hand crack at night," Bergeron said as we left the plant. Noticing a family searching for pecans in piles of leaves on the lawn next to the factory, I realized harvesting a small quantity was still a hand operation.

After purchasing nuts and pecan candy from Bergeron's office/outlet store, I decided this was Christmas shopping at its best: no snow, no crowds, and the added benefit of beautiful scenery along the western edge of the False River.

Best time to go:

The False River area is pretty any time of year, but I like to visit in November and December when both the sugarcane and the pecan crops are harvested.

Bergeron Pecan Shelling Plant

Hwy. 1
New Roads, LA 70760
(504) 638-7667

Pointe Coupee Parish

Office of Tourism
Louisiana Hwy. 1 South
HC 62, Box 70-M
New Roads, LA 70760
(504) 638-9858

Joe's "Dreyfus Store" Restaurant

Hwy. 77 South
Livonia, LA
(504) 637-2625

English Louisiana

SOUTHERN HOSPITALITY: TOURING HISTORIC HOUSES

HOW TO GO:

I-10 to Baton Rouge, follow signs to U.S. 110 , then to U.S. 61 north. For St. Francisville turn west on Hwy. 10. Rosedown Plantation is to the east on LA 10; Butler Greenwood House and Catalpa Plantation are north of St. Francisville on U.S. 61, and Oakley House is east on LA 965. Rosedown and Oakley House (Audubon State Park) are well-marked.

CATALPA PLANTATION

9508 U.S. Hwy. 61
St. Francisville, LA 70775
(504) 635-3372

BUTLER GREENWOOD HOUSE

8345 U.S. Hwy. 61
St. Francisville, LA 70775
(504) 635-6312

ROSEDOWN PLANTATION

12501 LA Hwy. 10
St. Francisville, LA 70775
(504) 635-3110

OAKLEY HOUSE AT AUDUBON STATE PARK

11788 LA Hwy. 965
St. Francisville, LA 70775
(504) 635-3739

Pioneered by well-heeled planters in the early nineteenth century, the quiet river town of St. Francisville is the heart of "English" Louisiana: a bastion of High Church Protestantism, of antebellum ostentation, and a modern tourist attraction. The town has more than 140 structures on the National Register within its two-mile-long historic district and there are ten plantation homes open to the public year-round. Between them the great homes hold enough hand-wrought silver, Sevres china, and New Orleans made furniture to fill a wing of the Metropolitan Museum of Art.

With so much history to choose from, it must have been hard for the local historical society to focus on one period for its major promotional event—The Audubon Pilgrimage—held annually in spring to commemorate the visit of artist James J. Audubon to St. Francisville more than 40 years before the outbreak of the Civil War. Another well-attended special event is the Southern Garden Symposium and Workshops, held in fall and—like the Pilgrimage—featuring access to several private properties. However, there's no need to wait for a special event to visit St. Francisville. Whenever you go, there will be more old homes than you can see comfortably in one or even two days. I spent a full day, saw four plantations, strolled through downtown St. Francisville and by evening, found myself footsore, but fascinated, and ready to visit again.

The rolling hills and tall hardwood forests of West Feliciana Parish are more akin to East Coast horse-country than Louisiana's slow bayous and mysterious swamps. In fact many of the planters who founded St. Francisville came from the Carolinas, carving out immense acreages of cotton, sugarcane, and indigo and establishing a refined eastern-style social life to match.

One such land owner was Daniel Turnbull of Rosedown Plantation who expressed his wealth in a pillared plantation home surrounded by 28 acres of meticulously kept gardens. Today Rosedown is still the area's preeminent plantation, but it has become one of the most commercial as well. An expensive, briskly paced tour takes you through the treasure-filled house. Then you are free to roam the sculpture-studded garden paths as long as you'd like. For an extra fee you can purchase a history of Rosedown or watch a film in the gift shop.

While the extensive gardens and lavishly restored Greek Revival house at Rosedown might be considered the area's showplace, the heart and soul of St. Francisville—and centerpiece of the Pilgrimage—is clearly Oakley House, the plantation where

Audubon taught the daughter of the house for four months in 1821.

Deep in the wooded park where Audubon stalked and painted some 32 birds during his stay, Oakley rises a cool, unencumbered three stories in height. It was patterned after the homes of the West Indies, raised to catch the merest breeze, with a shady, louvered sleeping porch and gallery for quiet repose. You can visit Oakley year-round. It is part of the state park system. For a small fee you get an informative tour, and an unlimited stay on the grounds where there are numerous out-buildings.

Every house in the small community of St. Francisville adds at least one puzzle part to the picture of nineteenth-century life, but Mamie Thompson's Catalpa Plantation has more than its share.

Thompson's personal tour focused on the contents of her raised Victorian cottage, built in 1855 on the site of the family's earlier grand house. The tour began at a shelf full of treasures just inside the front door. There, I saw miniatures and photos of Thompson's mother, a true southern belle who had grown up at nearby Rosedown plantation, and other relatives who had hailed from Audubon's onetime residence, Oakley House.

Many of the rare objects within were brought to Catalpa when the family relinquished its hold on Rosedown. Others, like the silver that survived the Civil War in a burlap sack on the bottom of the plantation's lake, had been there since part of Thompson's family came to St. Francisville from the Carolinas in the early 1800s. Thompson often ends her tour with a glass of sherry and a few pleasant moments of visiting. It's a grand opportunity to knit together the myriad genealogical tidbits one hears on various house tours, while sampling real southern hospitality.

Tour Butler Greenwood Plantation or stay the night: five modern bed and breakfast cottages are spread out on the property behind the 1795 plantation home.

I ended my day in St. Francisville on the front porch of another descendant of the town's earliest settlers. The Butler Greenwood House, begun in 1796, is screened from traffic along Highway 61 by a park of live oaks, also two centuries old.

Open to the public only since the early 1990s, Butler Greenwood House retains the feel of a private home while operat-

The grand dame among St. Francisville's many plantation homes, Rosedown still bears a black mourning stripe painted in the nineteenth century when a son of the family died an untimely death.

Audubon Pilgrimage

The Pilgrimage is held the third weekend in March. Bed and breakfast homes throughout the St. Francisville area are booked early for Pilgrimage weekend. Last minute pilgrims may still find accommodations in nearby Milbank, New Roads, Jackson, and Baton Rouge. Pilgrimage headquarters is behind Market Hall. For information call the West Feliciana Historical Society (504) 635-6330. A light Pilgrimage lunch is sold at Jackson Hall.

ing as a professionally run bed and breakfast. Anne Butler, a seventh generation resident of the house, built private guest cottages only steps away from her plantation home. Each of these five modern "dependencies," has a different setting and decor.

Butler gives the house tour herself, highlighting the family's remarkable collections of Mardi Gras invitations, nineteenth century clothing and china. All this is mixed with her own twentieth-century belongings.

One room which shows no sign of the twentieth century is the formal parlor, decorated with a rare twelve-piece matching set of Victorian rosewood furniture in its original upholstery. Framed on the wall is a bill of sale for $467.05 from a Bridgeport, Connecticut furniture maker and a follow-up letter dating from the early days of the Civil War that requests speedy payment despite, "the difficult time in our country."

In the dining room hangs a painting of Harriet Flower Mathews, a long-lived nineteenth-century relative whose records provided Louisiana State University researchers with a picture of life in the house both before and after the Civil War. "I used her records for my tour," said Butler who noted that her ancestor planted the oaks that surround Grace Episcopal Church in St. Francisville.

I'd seen those oaks earlier on a walking tour of St. Francisville's historic district. But even after a day learning about the families of four plantations, I'd barely begun to discover the town's past. And even if I had learned all the history, I would not have exhausted the fun of this area. Whether you see the town by walking tour, bicycle or hot air balloon—all these are options in St. Francisville—be sure to allow plenty of time for exploration.

St. Francisville — Audubon Pilgrimage

During the Audubon Pilgrimage in spring (March) one tour ticket buys access to a selection of the town's public and private architectural treasures. Four private homes, three churches, two gardens, a state park, and a historic re-creation called Rural Homestead are typical offerings. The ticket also includes free admission to a theatrical performance and musical evenings at area churches.

Each year different private homes are featured on the tour but one thing doesn't change: townspeople at every pilgrimage stop are dressed in elaborate costumes from the 1820s made by local seamstresses. The care taken to duplicate authentic costumes from Audubon's era is most impressive.

My favorite pilgrimage stop is Afton Villa Gardens, a restored classical garden built around the ruins of the Barrow family's 40 room Gothic mansion. Daffodil Valley, part of the gardens, contains nearly 100,000 blooms in March. Elsewhere you will find 11,000 colorful tulips and 13,000 pansies.

Afton Villa Gardens is open seasonally.

JACKSON, LOUISIANA

A lovely, much-less-visited town in East Feliciana Parish is Jackson. Home of historic Centenary College, this small, walkable town features many Greek Revival, Victorian, and Colonial houses. Names and dates are highlighted on markers. The Jackson museum contains a diorama of a nearby Civil War battle, a large display of miniature lead soldiers and loads of local memorabilia.

On a short length of track behind the museum, is the work of railroad enthusiast Leroy Harvey: A handsome string of excursion cars and a steam engine decked with a cowcatcher await more narrow gauge track and funding. Another of Harvey's projects, the Feliciana Cellars winery, opened in March 1994. Here you can taste several varieties of muscadine grape wine, tour the factory, and purchase everything from muscadine juice to jam.

I tried Bear Corners restaurant when I visited Jackson and was rewarded with a very fine meal. The chef is the brother of Joe, of Joe's "Dreyfus Store" Restaurant in Livonia.

JACKSON

FELICIANA CELLARS
1848 Charter Street
P.O. Box 369
Jackson, LA
(504) 634-7982

BEAR CORNERS
1674 Charter Street
Jackson, LA 70748
(504) 634-2844

HOW TO GO:
From St. Francisville follow Hwy. 10 northeast to Jackson.

Ride the rails in Jackson? Not yet. This train waits behind the town museum, as plans are drawn for an excursion line through the wooded hill country of East Feliciana Parish.

Nottoway Plantation

RIVER ROAD'S LARGEST PLANTATION HOME DESIGNED FOR ROMANCE

How to go:
The fast way is I-10 west, exit LA 22, then LA 70 across the Sunshine Bridge. North 14 miles on Hwy. 1. A less-travelled way with opportunities for interesting side trips starts on New Orleans' west bank. Take Hwy. 90 to 3127. Continue north through Donaldsonville until you see the sign for Nottoway.

BEST TIMES TO GO:
Nottoway is one of River Road's most popular house tours. Try early in the morning or call ahead to avoid the tour buses.

NOTTOWAY PLANTATION
P.O. Box 160
White Castle, LA 70788
9 AM - 5 PM
By admission: $$
(504) 545-2730

"Just don't go to bed mad," counseled Mrs. Owens, the octogenarian former owner, and resident-for-life of Nottoway Plantation. She dispensed her marital philosophy to some newlyweds who drifted into her doll shop in the basement of the River Road mansion. Owens, a former teacher, came to Nottoway at age 40 when she married its owner, the high school principal.

"Ours was a late marriage, but a very happy one. I lost my husband in '74 and I've missed him every day since then," she said.

After hearing the story of Nottoway, I understood that marital counseling fit right in: the mansion was built to attract suitors for the eight marriageable daughters of Virginia-born sugar planter John Hampden Randolph. Neighbors scoffed when Randolph built the entirely white ball room and elegant music room to showcase the girls, but the sheer size and magnificence of the River Road home impressed all comers, and the girls were quickly married.

Nottoway's 50 rooms, 200 windows and 65-foot ballroom were also the result of a friendly competition between Randolph and another River Road Virginian, John Andrews. Ignoring the prospect of a war with the northern states, the two set out to "one-up" each other by building the grandest houses the River Road had ever seen. They utilized the latest technology in plumbing and gas-lighting, and vied over decorative details: Nottoway's doorknobs were hand-painted Dresden porcelain, and Belle Grove's were real silver. In the end, Andrew's Belle Grove surpassed Nottoway for a total of 70 rooms, and the five daughters of the rival house were also married off. Then came the war.

A favored honeymoon spot, the "dependency" at Nottoway is larger than most honeymooner's first homes. The main house contains 16 fireplaces and 200 windows.

Miraculously neither plantation was destroyed, though Nottoway had a close call and still shows the marks of shots fired at its stately pillars. As the story goes, cannon fire was stopped by order of a Union officer who remembered the Randolphs' gracious pre-war hospitality. After the Civil War, extravagant plantation lifestyles were difficult to maintain and both homes passed through a succession of owners.

Belle Grove eventually fell into disrepair and was razed, but Nottoway was preserved by the Owens family who bought it at auction in 1911. After Mrs. Owens was widowed, she sold it to a Baton Rouge preservationist who restored and opened the property to the public.

Though only two rooms have the original furnishings, Nottoway provides a good example of River Road prosperity at its peak. One room is entirely decorated with 1830s wicker furniture brought to Nottoway from Mrs. Randolph's childhood home in Mississippi. Original plasterwork friezes and ceiling medallions are matched by copies of period draperies, furniture, and colors.

Though the tour guides too frequently remind visitors that Nottoway is now a bed and breakfast, some aspects of the accommodations are of interest. Every guest, whether they stay in the main house, the original garconniére, or one of the "transplanted" out buildings is given a key to the house and encouraged to use it as their home for the evening. I imagined dancing in the moonlight in the all-white ball room, but couldn't help thinking about the widow Randolph leaving Nottoway for the last time. After her husband's death she is said to have closed each of the two hundred windows in the house, descended the grand staircase in a sweeping black gown and left without looking back.

On the Way — Donaldsonville

I eyed the flower bed on Louisiana Square, seeking a vantage from which to photograph the stately nineteenth-century courthouse in downtown Donaldsonville. Suddenly the flower bed's custodian and representative of the town's historical society approached me and pointed to the side of the square.

"Care to see the photos in our little museum house?" she asked. I'd overlooked the tiny frame building, which seemed to be undergoing renovation. "We've always called it the little pink house and now I suppose, we'll have to refer to it as the little red house," said my guide as she led me through the front door, negotiating ladders and cans of red paint.

Inside I saw that the tiny house was once the office of a Dr. Lowery, a black physician who served the integrated community just after the Civil War. Other than Dr. Lowery's picture and diploma, the old doctor's office was devoted to historic photographs of Donaldsonville's houses and public buildings. Most still stand and can be located by visitors. One photo shows flood waters lapping the steps of a building now standing safely behind the pumping station near the levee. A free guide to the historic district and several good local cookbooks are available for sale in the house.

HOW TO GO:
Take I-10 to exit 182. Cross the Sunshine Bridge on Hwy. 70 and bear right (north) on Hwy. 1 to Donaldsonville. (I was told that the Sunshine Bridge—brainchild of one time Governor Jimmy Davis—spanned the Mississippi only to end in a sugarcane field. It's true, but falsely implies the bridge leads nowhere. In fact, it leads to a spaghetti bowl of roads that, once untangled, become the way to Donaldsonville, Louisiana.)

The courthouse in Donaldsonville, seat of Ascension Parish. For one year, the city was the state capitol of Louisiana.

This rare Doric-Greek and Egyptian Revival tomb in Donaldsonville's Catholic cemetery is thought to be designed by James Dakin, architect of the Old State Capitol building in Baton Rouge.

My new friend offered to lend a more extensive history of the town if I would follow her home. We drove past a row of shotgun houses, several interesting churches, and along a line of increasingly elegant bayou-side homes until we reached her house, where she searched for the town's printed history. While waiting, I studied her collection of blue and white china arrayed on the walls.

My guide was a great impromptu ambassador for Donaldsonville, and her history, once found, was full of interesting facts including the following:

—William Donaldson, the real estate speculator who planned the town, succeeded, albeit posthumously, in moving the state capitol from New Orleans to Donaldsonville for one year (1830-1831). The legislators complained that Government House (no longer standing) was too cold and drafty and returned to the Ursuline Convent in New Orleans.

—In addition to its Acadian immigrants, the Donaldsonville area received a large number of Sicilian immigrants in the 1890s. It's easier to find an Italian restaurant in Donaldsonville than a fast food franchise. Ruggerios, the Railroad Cafe, and the Last Chance were recommended by my guide.

—B. Lemann & Brothers Inc., Louisiana's first department store, is still operating as a hardware, seed and feed store on Mississippi Street. The three-story brick building, was designed by New Orleans architect James Freret, for Jacob Lemann, a one-time peddler who began his career travelling the river parishes. With its cast iron gallery and rich ornamentation, the structure is a nearly perfect example of an Italianate commercial building.

—During two different epidemics the Jewish Cemetery in Donaldsonville accepted yellow fever victims from overcrowded New Orleans. The town's cemeteries are full of nineteenth-century tombs and are worth exploring.

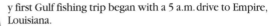
Gulf Fishing

OFFSHORE PLATFORMS
LURE ANGLERS

HOW TO GO:
Take the Crescent City
Connection to LA 90
then exit on Hwy. 23.
Drive south to Empire—
about 1 1/2 hours.

BEST TIME TO GO:
June through October are best for all
species offshore. Marsh fishing for
inshore species is good year-round.

*Louisiana anglers
have great big
reasons to smile.*

My first Gulf fishing trip began with a 5 a.m. drive to Empire, Louisiana.

Thanks to Dramamine and the early hour, I dozed, awakening once to the sound of a leviathan sliding into the ice locker next to my head. The next time the excited voices of my fishing companions roused me as they hauled a big fish toward the boat.

"Wake up and get the camera," they yelled between effort-filled grunts. I peered at them through a fogged wide angle lens while they hauled the flapping 20-pound redfish aloft, grinning triumphantly at the world. Gulf fishing makes for some interesting napping, but by now I was determined to stay awake.

Following the captain's advice, I searched for a distant focal point, hoping to calm my stomach. No land in sight; those bobbing oil platforms would have to do. Anchored to horizontal pipes at the base of the platform with something that looked like a shepherd's crook, our boat held in the current where fish like to congregate, attracted by the lights and structure of the platform. I tried to keep my footing while baiting the hook. We were rig fishing with spinning tackle and 25-pound test line, using shrimp for bait.

Catching fish proved to be relatively easy, but letting them go again would have been impossible for me without help. All sorts of unfamiliar teeth, fins, and whiskers came out of the Gulf that day: spadefish, lemonfish, redfish, cobia, gafftopsail catfish, and zebra-striped sheepshead that looked like they had escaped someone's aquarium. They banged around on the deck of our 20-foot sport fishing boat until my friends unhooked and returned them to the sea.

That day the Gulf looked like choppy chocolate milk. Dark clouds gathered to the south, so we moved from one rig to another, seeking new fish and dodging cloudbursts on the way. The 20-foot boat could handle the chop, but our captain prudently stayed close enough to shore to make a run for it if the weather turned really bad. When I grew tired of fishing, I tried to make sense out of the static and garbled Louisiana accents on the VHF radio. Strange voices came out of the ether, some complained of slow fishing, others warned wayward boaters to "watch that squall on your tail."

It could not have been a slow day fishing everywhere though, because several fully-loaded menhaden boats passed us on their way back into port. Empire is one of the largest commercial fishing ports in Louisiana for shrimp and menhaden, a small fish that's crushed for its oil.

About 4 p.m. the weather finally drove us back to shore. The day ended with a fruitless attempt at fly fishing in brackish marsh water that yielded nothing more than a closeup view of a raccoon gazing dreamily at mullet leaping beyond its reach. We admired the sunset from a shell midden for a while, rode in past a boneyard of old shrimp boats, and took our place in the cue of tired boaters waiting their turn for the pull-out crew.

It was said to be a slow day for fishing, but I enjoyed all of it including the nap and the fish dinner for six that ended the day.

I went with a private party, but several charter services operate out of Empire and nearby Venice. Some fish near the gas and oil platforms ten to twelve miles from shore as we did, others troll for tarpon farther out in the blue water Gulf. I'd suggest calling first, describing the type of fishing experience you'd like, and chatting with the captain about rules and regulations of his charter. My captain was a good-natured sort who didn't care if I slept through half the action, as long as I was having fun. If you're a novice like me, sunscreen, Dramamine, and liquid refreshments are important, but compatible fishing companions are a must.

TOM'S PLACE IN EMPIRE – OYSTER HEAVEN ON THE HALF SHELL

For oyster lovers the real heart and soul of New Orleans cooking is an hour south of the French Quarter in the oyster beds of Plaquemines Parish, where Croatian oystermen have been harvesting the sea for over a hundred years.

We set out for Tom's Place in Empire, Louisiana, to eat our fill.

Shopping centers and fast-food joints gave way to rows of tiny orange trees and vegetable stands as we followed the Mississippi's west bank south to Port Sulphur. In December, during the Plaquemines Parish Orange Festival, roadside stands are loaded with oranges. In summer local families sell a variety of home-grown produce: fresh green okra, Creole tomatoes, preserved hot peppers, and eggplant. We filled our car and asked directions to Tom's. The vegetable man knew owner Tom Morovich, and knew

CHARTERS:

Several captains operate out of each marina. Call for details.

EMPIRE – DELTA MARINA
(504) 657-9726

VENICE MARINA
(504) 534-9357

TOM'S PLACE

Empire, LA
(504) 657-7766

HOW TO GO:

Follow the Crescent City Connection to LA 90 then exit on Hwy. 23. Follow 23 south until the highrise bridge just before Empire. Turn left before the bridge and follow the road into town. Tom's Place is on the left.

BEST TIME TO GO:

Call for hours. Business is slow and sporadic in Plaquemines Parish since the oil bust.

his dad and mom before him. "Nice family," he said directing us to the old highway.

Tom's Place has had floodwaters halfway up the walls several times, but you'd never know it from the spotless appearance of the

one-room restaurant. After the last hurricane, Morovich redecorated with new panelling and nets full of plastic fish, but the side bar with its row of padded bar stools has the same homey style it had when his father opened it in 1950.

Morovich served platters of oysters on the half-shell with all the fixings: lemon, horseradish, Tabasco, olive oil, and ketchup. Of all the combinations lemon juice, salt, and

Tom's Place, close to Empire's oyster beds, has satisfied seafood lovers for decades.

olive oil got our vote. We ate dozens of raw oysters then tried the gumbo and a variety of seafood—including more oysters, fried in a fluffy cornmeal batter. Tom's oysters were fresh and salty, and Morovich pried them open lightning fast, even opening some behind his back.

No newcomer to the oyster business, Morovich proudly displays the second-place award he won for shucking oysters in a 1988 oyster festival. "My wife and I went there just to see it and she talked me into competing. The guy who beat me by one second went on to win the National Oyster Championships."

Like other area Croatians, Morovich's father had been an oysterman before he opened his restaurant. "You can't do both things well," said Morovich. "We still have the beds, but lease them to other oystermen." He told us how seed oysters are obtained from the state, then placed west of Plaquemines Parish where heavy waterflow from the Gulf provides plenty of nutrients to grow large oysters and salty water improves their flavor.

But are they a safe, year-round treat?

"Years ago people came up with the idea of never eating oysters in a month that has no 'r' in the name, but that was when there was no refrigeration and transportation was slow. That and the fact that oysters are milky in the summer months, scares a lot of people off. We've never had any bad incidents down here and we've been serving oysters for 40 years," said Morovich.

Fort Jackson

Hurricanes, oil prices, fishing conditions, and politics make life in Plaquemines Parish as unstable as the land which lies between its levees. Even the fate of national historic landmark Fort Jackson, near the Mississippi's mouth, is in question, its funding the subject of political battles. Though cut back from fourteen to five employees, the fort is open to visitors seven days a week and hundreds come to walk the spacious compound and old brick ramparts.

The 60-mile drive from New Orleans to Fort Jackson is more interesting when it's broken by a river crossing or two. I explored the less-travelled east bank of the Mississippi, crossing on one of Plaquemines Parish's free ferries at Belle Chasse and driving south along the levee to Pointe a la Hache. The road takes you past several notable plantations: both the Perez property and Mary Plantation are lovely buildings in lush settings. Today most of the cultivated areas are planted with tiny orange trees and vegetables but in the late 1800s Plaquemines was the primary source for rice in the state.

Just before the road ended I came to the parish seat of Pointe a la Hache and another ferry crossing. In the center of that tiny town stood the county courthouse, the tallest brick building I'd seen since leaving Belle Chasse.

Court was in session as I tiptoed through the second floor courtroom to catch a sweeping view of the river from the base of the bell tower. Uniformed deputies stood around the courthouse, attorneys conducted business over cellular phones on the courthouse steps, and everyone else lined up in chairs against the walls beneath historic photos of Plaquemines Parish, or hung out at the sandwich shop down the block.

ROAD SOUTH LEADS TO ORANGE GROVES, OYSTERS, AND OLD FORT

DOWNRIVER 1 to 2 HOURS

HOW TO GO:

Take the Crescent City Connection to LA 90, then exit at LA 23. Pass through the tunnel on 23 and turn left at the Belle Chasse ferry landing sign. Cross the river and follow Hwy. 39 south. Recross at Pointe a la Hache and continue south on 23. Fort Jackson is four miles south of Buras. Miljak's Restaurant is on the west side of LA 23 in Empire.

FORT JACKSON

P. O. Box 7043
Buras, LA 70041
Open seven days
9 AM - 4 PM
Free admission, but donations are accepted.
(504) 657-7083

Once half-submerged and infested with snakes, Fort Jackson and its contents were dried out and displayed. A museum of military memorabilia is filled with objects found at the fort.

A reversed image of Woodland Plantation has long graced bottles of Southern Comfort whiskey.

It was a quiet, uneventful day in Pointe a la Hache, and the west bank bustled with commerce in comparison. When I recrossed the Mississippi River by ferry, I found seafood restaurants, several big commercial marinas, a bed and breakfast, and more car traffic.

I stopped for lunch at newly rejuvenated Miljak's in Empire, for years a mainstay for west bank travelers. When owner Bubby Sercovich redecorated, he made use of his considerable maritime knowledge to rebuild the interior with sections of boats: an oyster lugger bow holds the cash register and a brightly painted wheelhouse encloses a bathroom. The food was nicely prepared and the restaurant was cheery and comfortable. Sercovich sat down at my table and crossed his arms, baring his many tattoos. "I grew up across the river where there were no roads and going to school meant going by boat. I've done just about everything: worked on oyster luggers, crewboats, and tugboats," he said. He builds model boats too, and before I headed down the road for Fort Jackson, he showed me several that had careful detailing, tiny oyster rakes and moving parts.

Everyone I met in Plaquemines Parish seemed to have time for hobbies, including Fort Jackson's director, Sarah McKee. Her one time hobby of coin collecting blossomed into a scholarly passion for the archeology of the fort, where she and her husband once hunted for coins with a metal detector.

"I made my first trip in here by pirogue," she said recalling that the site was once regularly flooded and infested with snakes.

Eventually the couple found so many artifacts it led to Fort Jackson's excavation and preservation. McKee built a small museum within the fort walls, its cases filled with telltale evidence of military life. She showed me an unopened sardine can that had been found in the moat and a Civil War mini-ball flattened for a poker chip. "I guess Louisianians always liked to gamble," McKee commented.

Like every past occupant of the fort, McKee and her staff are constantly fighting water. She has evacuated the collection for hurricanes more times than she can remember, and the nearby Mississippi River is still a threat despite a protective levee built in the 1960s. "All our forts have been lost to the river because the river wants to straighten out," said McKee.

I pondered McKee's comment as I strolled on the star-shaped ramparts and peered into massive tunnels beneath the fort's walls. When Fort Jackson surrendered to Admiral Farragut during the Civil War, it had less to do with inadequate armaments than with hostile elements: It was exceptionally wet and cold that year and everyone in the fort was sick from malaria. Even if they had been able to man their guns, their powder was wet. Farragut—"damn Yankee" said McKee —simply waited on Ship Island until the river was up and the inhabitants were helpless.

As I drove upriver I came across another Plaquemines Parish landmark with an unusual past and an uncertain future. Woodland Plantation, long-pictured on Southern Comfort bottles, lies in ruins just north of Port Sulphur. No comfort for southern history buffs already concerned by cutbacks at Fort Jackson.

EMPIRE — BRINGING IN THE OYSTER CATCH

From the highrise bridge above Empire, I saw oyster luggers returning with the day's catch. The sunset view encompassed miles of water, marshes, and hundreds of brightly colored boats. Plaquemines Parish produces some of America's best-tasting oysters—and I wanted a closer look at the industry. From Empire, I followed a winding, shell-covered road across the levee to a dock at Chris's Exxon, where luggers heavy with oysters tied up at the dock to off-load their catch. Wind-burned workers in white shrimpers' boots hefted sacks onto conveyer belts that led to refrigerated trucks.

Captain "Skinny" stood by the conveyer belt tagging more than a hundred sacks with the date and location of the catch. A handsome man with a thick Croatian accent, Skinny explained that 20 years of oystering had been good to him. When he came from Dubrovnik, he was the fourth generation in his family to dredge oysters in Plaquemines Parish. Now he has two boats. "But then, I'm still single and no one is spending my money." He pointed to a wooden boat, neatly painted and an obvious object of pride. "We used to call it the 'Yugoslavia'. But now there is no country of Yugoslavia so we call it the 'Skinny'." His friend, oyster broker Paul Pelas, came out of the office to show us a beautifully carved miniature of Skinny's boat that he had made for Skinny.

It seemed that oysters aren't the only reason to visit Plaquemines Parish—the people are just as nice.

An oyster lugger returns home loaded with oysters from Plaquemines Parish beds.

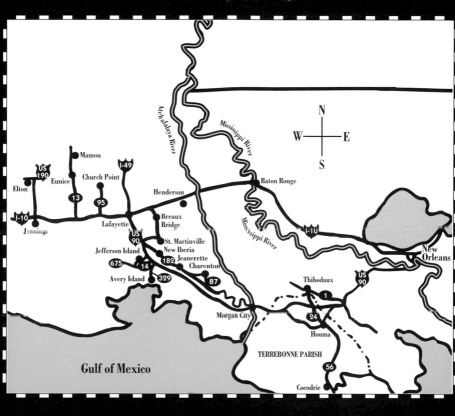

Tabasco Factory and Jungle Gardens

NATURALLY HOT ATTRACTIONS SHOWCASE LOUISIANA CUISINE AND CREATURES

HOW TO GO:

I-10 to Lafayette, then U.S. 90 south through Lafayette to New Iberia. At LA 14, exit and turn left. At the junction of LA 329 turn right and continue until you reach Avery Island.

BEST TIME TO GO:

Try an early afternoon tour, then spend the rest of the day in Jungle Gardens.

Camellias bloom from November to March.

Azaleas bloom from February to late April.

Egrets nest from March to July.

The peppers used to make the first Tabasco sauce came from Mexico, but the McIlhenny Company's continuous selection for color and flavor has resulted in a distinct botanical species of pepper.

What comes in a bottle with a trademark diamond label, red octagonal cap, and green-banded neck? Diners the world over know that the answer is Tabasco, conceivably Louisiana's best-known export after jazz. And just as the historic jazz sites of New Orleans attract pilgrims, so too does Avery Island, home to the world's only Tabasco factory—and a wildlife refuge established by the makers of the pungent red hot sauce.

The only road to Avery Island is a low, straight blacktop flanked by salt marshes on both sides. One hundred and fifty miles from New Orleans a tree-covered island rises in the distance—an oddity in the flat expanse of the Gulf Coast that seems even stranger when you learn that it is the tip of a salt mountain taller than Mount Everest.

Only the parts of Avery Island that house the Tabasco factory and a nature preserve called Jungle Gardens are open to the public. The rest is a mixture of agricultural, industrial, and residential property, all kept meticulously groomed by the McIlhenny Company. It contains a section of worker housing that is over a hundred years old, fields of perfectly manicured pepper bushes, sugarcane, oil wells, a gigantic underground salt mine, and tree-screened homes for the McIlhennys and Averys who still reside there. The island has its own school, post office, and delicatessen.

I visited one afternoon when the sun was sinking into the red-speckled pepper fields. "After the last picking, we plow those under. McIlhenny's is like the Cajun saying: 'We use everything but the squeal'," said company spokesman Mike Morris. The first peppers Edmund McIlhenny mashed into sauce were grown from Mexican seeds, but over the years, the McIlhennys planted seeds of peppers with the best color and juice for Tabasco, resulting in a distinct botanical species of pepper. To meet today's demand for hot sauce, many of the peppers used are grown in South and Central America with seeds shipped from Avery Island Tabasco peppers.

At the factory you can see barrels of salted pepper mash aging in oak barrels like fine wine. The peppers are mashed the day they are picked, salted then aged up to three years. Later vinegar is added and the sauce is stirred periodically for a month before bottling. The tour ends at the Tabasco Country Store, which sells a line of Tabasco-related products, including numerous accessories decorated with crimson peppers.

I was struck by the fact that two of Tabasco's three ingredients, peppers and salt, are produced on Avery Island. Safety regulations prohibit public tours of the salt mine and it is a shame because the sight of 100-foot high, mile-wide tunnels below the earth must be astounding. The mine produces two million tons of salt per year. "Add the island's two other crops, sugarcane and oil, and we are the hottest, sweetest, saltiest, and oiliest island in the world," said Morris.

The island's 200 acre wildlife park, Jungle Gardens, disguises the nearby industrial activity. More than an exotic garden, the park is refuge to hundreds of bird species. It's easy to see the hand of its builder, naturalist Edmund McIlhenny, in the walls of bamboo, giant Buddha, alligator ponds, and bird-nesting platforms. You can see the park either by car or on foot, but I enjoyed it most on foot in late afternoon. Large white birds, many of them previously endangered species, filled the trees around the floating platform at "Bird City." I was alone in the observation tower, but the cries of the birds were almost deafening. It was hard to imagine the days when the egret was so endangered that McIlhenny searched the swamps until he found six to bring to this protected spot. Today they behave like the crowds of Tabasco fanciers, returning in greater numbers each year.

NEW IBERIA – KONRIKO RICE FACTORY

When rice crackers were all the rage, I munched on Konriko's version thinking they were made in Japan, despite the pillared plantation house on the label.

Then I moved to Louisiana and learned that Konriko is a '50s-style tradename for Conrad Rice Milling and Planting Company of New Iberia, Louisiana. On a visit to Konriko's factory, I learned the secret of their famous Wild Pecan Rice and other specialty products, but I never found the plantation house.

The first thing I learned at Konriko is that Wild Pecan Rice contains no nuts. Wild Pecan Rice is Konriko's patented name for a hybrid developed by Louisiana State University researchers from a long-grained Indonesian rice. This aromatic rice is only partially milled with about ten percent of the bran layers removed. The aroma that fills the air when it's cooking is distinctly pecan-like. Aromatic rice—Basmati is one example—is highly preferred in the Middle East, but much less known in this country.

MCILHENNY COMPANY
Avery Island, LA 70513
Factory tours:
Mon. - Fri.
9 AM - 4 PM
Sat. 9 AM - noon
Closed Sundays and some long weekends. Admission free.
(318) 365-8173

JUNGLE GARDENS
9 AM - 5 PM
By admission: $$
(318) 369-6243

While connoisseurs identify Avery Island with Tabasco, hundreds of birds know the island and its Jungle Gardens as a safe spot to roost.

Wild Pecan Rice was one of many innovations made by Mike Davis who purchased the company from the Conrad family in 1975.

The Conrad Rice Milling and Planting Company started in 1912, making it the oldest rice mill in the nation. When the mill building was placed on the National Historic Register, Davis realized the tourist potential of the old facility and added the Company Store next door. Designed to look like an old general store from Louisiana's plantation era, the Company Store attracts between 30 to 40 thousand tourists a year. Local foods, cooking utensils, and Cajun crafts fill the shelves along with Konriko's products. A tour of the rice mill includes a short film on Cajun life and a taste of Cajun cuisine.

On the tour I watched as dried stalks of rice were unloaded from trucks marked Rayne or Crowley—towns in rice-growing country. The drivers were farmers too: their sunburned faces crinkled up into big smiles when someone asked them if they grew brown rice as well as white rice. White rice *is* brown rice, fully milled to remove the outer coating.

On some days you can see the sheller, pearler, tumbler, and grader at work, but on my visit a model was used to represent the process. The tour ended back in the Company Store where area cooks offered rice recipes and trouble-shooting advice over a cup of gumbo.

KONRIKO COMPANY STORE

P.O. Box 10640
New Iberia, LA 70562
Mon. - Sat. 9 AM - 5 PM
Tours 10 AM ,11 AM, 1 PM, 2 PM & 3 PM
(318) 367-6163
By admission: $

HOW TO GO:

From Lafayette take I-90 south to New Iberia. After you get into town follow Hwy. 14 to St. Peter St. (Hwy. 182). Right on St. Peter and right again on Ann Street. The mill is on your left.

BEST TIME TO GO:

Visit Konriko when you have time to see Shadows-on-the-Teche plantation home or Trappey's Fine Foods in New Iberia.

Chitimacha Indian Baskets

ouisiana's Chitimacha Indians still stand tall but their baskets are shrinking. A shortage of the mature three-to-five-year-old swamp cane from which they are woven has forced today's weavers to think small. In recent years the number of active weavers has dropped from six to three. Fearing a Native American tragedy, I decided to visit the Chitimacha reservation on Bayou Teche before the baskets disappeared altogether.

The Chitimacha Reservation's 283 acres don't look like the vast prairie reservations I was used to visiting in the West. Just a two-hour drive from New Orleans in St. Mary Parish, where rambling old river towns dot the reservation, the reservation resembles a well-kept suburb of green lawns and modest homes. There is a baseball diamond, picnic area, a drive-in restaurant, two gift shops, a small, modern visitor center and Louisiana's only federally funded Indian school.

A pervasive quiet yields few clues to this culture's impressive past. The Chitimacha were a powerful and peaceful tribe, dominating a huge area of swamp and bayou in southern Louisiana. They had plenty to eat and little reason to fight with others until European intervention. The culture was rich in arts of peacetime leisure: cooking, storytelling, and of course, craftwork. What other people would have time to painstakingly weave baskets that can last over 200 years?

Museums around the world display Chitimacha baskets in their collections. Their elaborate patternings and unusual double weave—two layers woven tightly enough to hold water—were once prized among Native American tribes who traded them across the continent.

The visitor center's collection of old and rare baskets, Chitimachan clothing, photographs, and other artifacts of historical interest paints a picture of a people closely linked to nature. Dark-eyed park ranger, Jody Basque, pointed out "worm tracks," "black-bird eyes," "alligator entrails," and other traditional patterns in the

BASKETS HOLD PAST AND FUTURE FOR LOUISIANA TRIBE

HOW TO GO:
Hwy. 90 to Morgan City. From here you can take either 90 or the old scenic Hwy. 182 which follows the river. Just north of Franklin on Hwy. 182 follow Hwy. 87 four miles into the reservation. A sign marks the turn.

BEST TIME TO GO:
Call the visitor center before you go. Hours are irregular.

VISITOR CENTER
Chitimacha Unit,
Jean Lafitte National Historical Park
3287 Chitimacha Trail
P.O. Box 609
Charenton, LA 70523
Admission free.
(310) 923-4030

Chitimacha Indian baskets are so tightly woven they were once used to transport water.

THE CHITIMACHA CRAFT SHOP

3592 Chitimacha Trail
Charenton, LA 70523
(318) 923-7547

NIX CRAFTS

3626 Chitimacha Trail
Charenton, LA 70523
(318) 923-4222

Clothing, baskets, and other Chitimacha artifacts are on display in the reservation's Visitor Center at Charenton.

baskets' black, red and ochre-chequered weavings. She told me about growing up on the reservation, the all-but-lost Chitimachan language, and the struggle to keep the weaving tradition alive.

The shortage has nothing to do with the demand for the baskets but rather the months and years it takes to learn the craft. The two newest weavers, John and Scarlett Darden, each had the advantage of a grandmother who was a weaver but they're adding to their knowledge by researching and duplicating the old, almost lost patterns. When I visited, the Dardens were delivering a new pattern they'd mastered to the sale case at the visitor center. No one had been able to teach them to make the pleasing heart-shaped basket, but they'd managed to "re-invent" the technique. Like most of the other baskets for sale at the visitor center, this basket was small—about the size of a swallow's nest. Today's baskets range from two to eight inches in diameter. The old ones were often much larger, but back then there was taller cane, more weavers, and more time for weaving.

The baskets which cost about $20 per square inch are available for sale in the visitor center, or directly from the artists by special arrangement. The nearby Chitimacha Craft Shop wasn't open the day I visited, but proprietor Mrs. Faye Stouff is considered to be an authority on herbal healing and is owner of a large private collection of baskets and artifacts.

Just down the road at Nix Crafts, tribal historian Nick Stouff invites visitors into the craft shop adjoining his kitchen. He recounts the tribe's oral history, then shows his silver jewelry, ceremonial artifacts, and a video about tribal legends. Like everyone else I talked to on the reservation, Nick met my interest in his culture with genuine enthusiasm. He could have told stories for hours.

Courir du Mardi Gras

Want your king cake and the chance to eat it too? Try Church Point's rural Mardi Gras—scheduled for the Sunday before Mardi Gras—without giving up Fat Tuesday fun in New Orleans.

It's called Courir du Mardi Gras, and it means a wild horseback ride through the back roads of Cajun country, gathering gumbo ingredients for a community-wide party. The towns of Eunice, Mamou, Ville Platte, Basile, and Iota also celebrate Mardi Gras this way, but their rides occur on Fat Tuesday.

Like many of Louisiana's rural traditions, the purpose of Courir du Mardi Gras is to make a party with enough food and entertainment for all comers—so outsiders are welcome. It's also a show of manliness for the community's teenage boys, a chance for older riders to pass on local tradition, and a hoot for all who gather on Church Point's main street to watch the returning riders.

The Courir du Mardi Gras is an all day affair, especially for the 150 riders who saddle up before sunrise. In Church Point it's men only—eighteen and older—who disguise their identities and meet their captains at dawn. They form a rag tag group—men in women's clothing, jesters, and clowns riding wildly from farm to farm, followed by flatbed trucks and wagons blaring Cajun music.

"Horses enjoy this as much as the riders. They love it because there's music all the way. They dance to it," said Dr. R.L. Savoy, Church Point chiropractor and long-time Courir enthusiast.

The route is kept secret, but at each farmstead the routine is the same. The head captain asks permission to bring on his rowdy crew of Mardi Gras bandits. "Then the riders carry on with all kinds of monkeyshines and the farmer throws up a chicken or some sausage and they scramble for it," said Savoy.

Though some riders are 75 years old, it helps to be young and frisky. The first saddle-warming toddies are consumed at dawn and drinking continues throughout the day. Some riders dance on top of their horses or break into a gallop, sending bystanders running. Church Point's sheriff helps the ride captains maintain order by making sure no property is

CAJUN CARNIVAL: CHASING CHICKENS ON A WILD CROSS COUNTRY RIDE

CAJUN COUNTRY 1 to 3 HOURS

HOW TO GO:
Take I-10 past Lafayette to exit 92, Hwy. 95. Go north to the first red light and turn right on the Church Point-Opelousas highway. The Saddle Tramp Riding Club is on the left one half mile from the light.

BEST TIME TO GO:
You can see the riders depart from the Saddle Tramp about 7:00 AM—then you're on your own until early afternoon when they return. Dr. Savoy suggests having lunch at the club at 11:00 AM, then finding a spot on Church Point's main street by 1:30 PM to view the parade.

SADDLE TRAMP RIDING CLUB
1036 E. Abbey
Church Point, LA 70525
(318) 684-2739
Free admission.

When they say "POWER" they mean it. This parade marshall is in charge of seeing that order is kept: "No women on the wagons," he cried when a group of revelers pulled me aboard for the Courir du Mardi Gras.

Courir du Mardi Gras revelers saddle up and start drinking at dawn, then ride from farm to farm in search of gumbo ingredients. A man in women's dress is a common Cajun Mardi Gras disguise.

COURIR DU MARDI GRAS

Ride organizers and phone numbers often change from year to year, but in small towns a phone call will usually lead to the person you need. Try these for starters:

MAMOU
(318) 468-2300

VILLE PLATTE
(318) 799-2456

TEE MAMOU - IOTA
(318) 779-2456

EUNICE
(318) 457-6575

damaged and locking up anyone who breaks the "no roughhousing" rule.

"There are always a few bumps and scrapes every year, but we fix 'em up again," said Savoy. "A long time ago they decided to organize the Courir du Mardi Gras to keep the mischief under control. When I was a child, two masked riders stole away our school teacher. The kids cried, not knowing the teacher recognized her boyfriend's horse."

By early afternoon the riders regroup and parade through town. They make a fine sight, though many are coated with mud or tipping out of their saddles. Friends and neighbors eagerly await the returning riders, lining store fronts along main street.

The parade ends with the crowd closing behind the last rider and proceeding by car or on foot to the Saddle Tramp Riding Club, where a traditional Cajun feast awaits. While the riders were on the trail of gumbo ingredients, a crew prepared the dance hall and the rest of the food—boudin, gratins, sausage, beer, soft drinks, and even homemade cakes and pies. Gumbo is served, and the riders, with costumes torn and muddy but faces glowing with exhilaration, rejoin their families.

Last year I left around sunset, and one local said, "You're leaving too soon! You'll miss the fight. There's one every year. See those kids rocking that outhouse? Well if they tip it—all hell's going to break loose. One or two kids get arrested every year, but they let them out at dawn. It's a tradition."

FAT TUESDAY – COURIR DU MARDI GRAS IN CAJUN COUNTRY

Courir du Mardi Gras are becoming increasingly popular. The list, shown at left, isn't complete, since each year more towns revive their traditional celebrations. Many include Cajun dance parties and newer ones have added craft fairs as well. If you want to participate, call ahead to see if outsiders are allowed to ride.

A community-wide gumbo dinner and Cajun dance caps the Courir du Mardis Gras in Church Point.

Louisiana Universities Marine Consortium

From a glass-walled observation tower south of Cocodrie, I surveyed one hundred miles of Louisiana's threatened coastline, a sweeping vista of golden marsh grass, and tidal channels—birthplace for 96 percent of the Gulf's fish—and home to LUMCON, Louisiana Universities Marine Consortium.

I expected to see the shoreline shift after talking with Clayton Harpold, Director of Marine Education for the state-financed research center. "Louisiana is disappearing. The state loses one football field's worth of wetlands every thirty minutes," he said as we toured the huge modern complex of laboratories.

Built in 1977, this 65,000 square foot facility provides laboratory space, testing equipment, and a fleet of research vessels to the state's universities to explore Louisiana's wetlands. Though it's primarily used by researchers in academic disciplines ranging from engineering to microbiology, LUMCON's marsh, bay, and Gulf teaching programs reach beyond the university community to secondary school groups, Elderhostel participants and day trippers in groups of five or more.

There's less to do at LUMCON if you don't call ahead for a tour, but individual visitors can peruse the fish tanks in the visiting area, enjoy educational displays, and climb the 65 foot observation tower.

The tower is a good place for an overview of the giant x-shaped facility. Built on raised pilings and connected to a network of walkways and docks, the marine center literally brings the laboratory into the field. Two large research vessels, the 103 foot *Pelican* and the 58 foot *Acadiana*, bobbed in the water beneath the building's wings.

Researchers collect field specimens from the marsh, Terrebonne Bay, or the Gulf of Mexico, and return to the marine center's "wet wing." Here sea water is carried

SPECTACULAR VIEWS AND SCIENCE-IN-PROGRESS DRAW VISITORS TO GULF COAST LABORATORIES

HOW TO GO:
Although this is only 85 miles from New Orleans, it takes about 2 1/2 hours to get there. Take I-90 south and west to Houma, follow signs to Hwy. 56 and follow Bayou Terrebonne until you reach Cocodrie. LUMCON is clearly marked on the right.

LUMCON
Chauvin, LA 70344
Admission free.
Fee for pre-arranged group tours and field trips.
(504) 851-2800

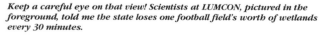
Keep a careful eye on that view! Scientists at LUMCON, pictured in the foreground, told me the state loses one football field's worth of wetlands every 30 minutes.

through overhead pipes to experiment stations, putting a controlled aquatic environment within reach of sophisticated computer and laser technology.

I saw many experiments in progress. One staffer adjusted the video reception from a microscope, studying the feeding behavior of day-old anchovy larvae; another monitored dead zones in the Gulf where decomposing organic material from the Mississippi River kills fish by depleting the oxygen. In the halls, researchers clad in rubber boots and foul weather gear checked weather charts on bulletin boards then disappeared through doorways that led down to the docks.

The labs also featured many special tools and study collections. I saw a tank shaped like a plexiglass race track that used lasers to measure the effect of currents on organisms; a collection room housed sea turtle bones, shark cartilage, and hundreds of other specimens in jars. "That's a favorite for visiting school children," said Harpold.

Other areas include a dormitory, apartments and a "dry wing," that houses a library, computers, and more laboratories. In the library I paged through a recent issue of ATOLL magazine and gazed over the serenity of the marsh through huge picture windows. Then Harpold brought me back to reality, noting that the dry wing wasn't always dry.

"Eighteen months after Hurricane Andrew we are still repairing damage from five feet of water in the lower floors," he said. "It's an interesting place to work."

LA TROUVAILLE RESTAURANT

La Trouvaille means "the lucky find" and patrons of this charming country eatery are lucky for two reasons: First is the authentic Cajun cooking; second, the warm family welcome extended to travellers.

La Trouvaille, located on Highway 56 south of Houma, looks like a favorite aunt's country home. Cars parked on the grass in front of the old wooden Cajun cottage reminded me of family gatherings with carloads of kids and casserole dishes. I instinctively skipped the front entry and headed for a side porch where rocking chairs flanked the kitchen door.

Inside everything was white and kitchen clean. The window above the kitchen sink was open to the trees and a balmy bayou breeze filled the room. Three of the four tables were surrounded by diners who ate so hungrily they hardly bothered to stop and talk. Each table was in a different stage of the day's fixed menu noon meal—red beans and rice, chicken gumbo, and pecan pie.

My meal began with homemade root beer and ended a full hour later with a generous helping of conversation with owner Wylma Duplantis Dusenbury.

LA TROUVAILLE
4696 Hwy. 56
Chauvin, LA 70344
(504) 594-9503 or (504) 873-8005.

HOW TO GO:
From Houma, drive south on Hwy. 56 five miles. The restaurant is on the right.

BEST TIME TO GO:
The restaurant is open for a noon meal on Wednesday, Thursday, Friday, and the first Sunday of every month. Closed in summer.

Chief chef and mother of twelve, Dusenbury begins her day at La Trouvaille at 4:30 a.m. with coffee, prayers, and a shopping list. "Because storage is limited, and because I really believe in doing things 'one day at a time', meals are planned and shopped for every morning." She also prepares a noontime dinner with live Cajun music on the first Sunday of every month. The music is provided by the Dusenbury family singers—an ensemble that was originally formed to sing thanks to friends and neighbors who helped the family through the births of three sets of twins.

At La Trouvaille Restaurant, Wylma Dusenbury will treat you to the same hearty Cajun lunch she learned to make for her twelve children.

Now that there are grandchildren and the family totals thirty-nine it's easy to see why there are never any leftovers at La Trouvaille. Reservations are encouraged simply to make sure there's enough food to go around.

Coushatta Indian Baskets

SEE ANTIQUE INDIAN BASKETS OR SHOP FOR NEW ONES

HOW TO GO:
I-10 past Lafayette to Jennings—about 2 1/2 hours from New Orleans. The Tupper Museum is at 311 Main Street. Turn south off I-10 on LA 26, then east on US 90 to Main Street and south to 311. (318) 821-5532

For Elton, take LA 97 north to US 190. Follow 190 west into Elton.

Bayou Indian Enterprises is on the north side of 190 just after you enter town. Baskets are also for sale on the Coushatta Reservation three miles north of Elton on Powell Road. (318) 584-2260. Lorena Langley can be contacted through Rosalene Medford (318) 584-2073.

BEST TIME TO GO:
Bert Langley at (318) 584-2653 organizes the Bayou Indian Festival in Elton on Father's Day weekend in June.

Lorena Langley, is one of fewer than twenty Coushatta Indian weavers who still make baskets.

f pine needle baskets shaped like turkeys and covered with pine cone "feathers" intrigue you, take a detour near Jennings, where the Coushatta Indians have been making such baskets since the 1700s. Warning: This is not an organized tourist attraction, but if you enjoy meeting the artists themselves, the area between Jennings and the Coushatta Reservation near Elton is a good place to explore.

I saw my first baskets unexpectedly in an old Jennings hardware store—now a museum—where the Coushattas traded baskets for food. Apparently there wasn't a going-out-of-business sale when W.H. Tupper General Merchandise closed in 1949. Ten thousand items, all in mint condition and many in their original boxes are still there. The Tupper Museum is fun to visit for a look at kewpie dolls, millinery, and high button shoes, and for a basket lover it's a gold mine. One of the largest known collections of antique Coushatta baskets is casually displayed along with the coffee grinders and kitchen implements, and can be examined without the glare of museum glass. Among them were cane baskets which are quite rare these days, and some of the largest longleaf pine baskets I've ever seen.

When the Coushatta or Koasati Indians moved to western Louisiana from Tennessee in the 1700s they brought their basket-making skills with them, but they couldn't bring the materials. Back East they wrapped sedge grass into coils with strips of slippery elm, but shortages of prairie grasses caused them to substitute the needles of longleaf pines that grew in abundance near their new home north of Elton, Louisiana. Makers chose imported African raffia over slippery elm in the early twentieth century and most weavers chose favorite tribal colors of red, black, white, and orange. Other tribes in Louisiana used cane for baskets and the Coushattta adapted their designs to this material too.

The earliest baskets were simple coiled trays or rounded shapes with tight-fitting lids. Some were decorated with stitched raffia flowers or pine cones, and others were made in the shapes of animals the Coushatta's admired. Only a few of the old baskets at The Tupper Museum replicated animals, but armadillos, geese, crawfish, bears, owls, alligators, and turkeys are among the animal effigy baskets made today.

At Elton, near the reservation, I learned more about the old baskets I'd seen in the Tupper Museum.

"Some of them are my grandmother's. She traded baskets for food at the Tupper store," said Bert Langley, owner of Bayou Indian Enterprises in Elton. "Today the demand for baskets is quite high because there are so few weavers and material is harder to get. Lumber companies are replacing longleaf pines with a faster-growing pine that has short needles. Also it's hard to get permission to gather needles on private land. We're trying to bring the prices up to help the weavers."

Animal effigy baskets are traditional among the Coushattas. This alligator basket simulates the beast's rough hide with pieces of pine cone.

Langley converted an old train depot into Bayou Indian Enterprises, filling it with a variety of Indian items from the Coushattas and other tribes. His small collection of baskets were perfectly uniform in shape and tightness. Prices ran about $10 per inch in diameter up to 10 inches and $15 per inch from 10 to 15 inches. Large ones are usually done on commission and can run up to $1800. I watched as Langley's soft-spoken mother sat perched on a stool in a long ruffled dress, minding the store while she worked on her latest basket.

There are fewer than twenty weavers among the Coushatta today. Two are men and they are the only ones who still make the cane baskets. I'd arranged in advance to visit one well-known weaver in her home on the edge of the reservation, and to my surprise it turned out to be Langley's aunt, sister of the woman in the store.

Lorena Langley, 61, shooed away the barking dogs when I honked my horn in front of her ramshackle home in the woods. She too was a woman of few words, but she told how the needles are picked wet then shaped into a coil when they are partially dry. Needles, pine cones, and raffia were piled on the table where she worked, old baskets hung on the wall, and a few partially finished crawfish and alligator baskets lay at hand. Her son's workbench had the beginnings of a cane basket.

Langley's work was as tidy and even as her sister's, but she was fashioning the needles into animal baskets. Their rounded shapes and lively expressions were inviting to the touch and have won much acclaim. The Smithsonian has several of her baskets in their collection. Animal effigies are central to the continuation of Coushatta culture. They illustrate the stories used to teach morals and pass oral history from one generation to another. Politeness and humility are among the lessons taught to Coushatta children.

When I asked Langley how she learned the craft, a long silence ensued. "My mother always made them...and we could learn from watching...but we weren't to ask questions because in our culture it is rude."

IN JENNINGS — THE ZIGLER MUSEUM

ZIGLER MUSEUM
411 Clara Street
Jennings, LA 70546
Tues. - Sat.
9 AM - 5 PM
Sun. 1 - 5 PM
By admission: $
(318) 824-0114

Wildlife dioramas, art glass, master paintings from America and Europe, and a sampling of duck decoys are part of the eclectic mix at the Zigler Museum of Jennings, Louisiana. One needs to look past inconsistencies in the collection, but there are a number of really fine pieces in this well-lit, professionally run small town institution. Among my favorites were a portrait head by French Impressionist Camille Pisarro; a nine-teenth-century seascape by George Innes; a domestic scene by Francois Millet; and a watercolor still life by Ellsworth Woodward—an artist whose work at Newcomb College in New Orleans helped define the look of American art pottery in the early twentieth century.

DONN E.'S COOKING

Jennings, Louisiana was settled by midwesterners around the turn-of-the-century, but the cooking of Cajun neighbors has had a major effect if one can judge by the food at Donn E.'s Restaurant. This simply appointed establishment is a favorite among local diners. While sampling the luncheon buffet, I saw the fire chief, an ambulance driver and a farmer in coveralls. The seafood was good and the service was fast and friendly. Open for breakfast, lunch, and dinner every day. Just north of I-10 on Highway 26.

Atchafalaya Levee

Speedboats raced my car's shadow as I crossed the twin bridges spanning the Atchafalaya Basin. Keeping one eye on the road, I watched the boats careening below me, dodging bridge abutments and spewing dark swamp water, then disappearing into the shadow of the eastbound lane.

Crossing the Atchafalaya Basin seems effortless from the air-conditioned comfort of an automobile. But I was mindful of the engineering feat that kept me on dry pavement as I glanced at the swamp spreading from horizon to horizon. The I-10 bridges parallel an earlier span—a railroad, now gone, that once stretched across 48 miles of swamp. The railroad lasted from 1907 to 1927 before flood waters swept it away. During those years, a town called Atchafalaya sprang up in the middle of the Basin before succumbing to the same fate as the railroad.

The people of Atchafalaya settled on the newly built levee near Henderson in the 1930s. The tiny fishing industry they brought with them supplied restaurants in nearby Henderson and Breaux Bridge. Today, the levee provides access to the Basin and support for recreational businesses.

Exiting I-10 at Henderson and making the first left took me past several restaurants. Both Las's and Robin's Restaurant were recommended by the locals: Las's for crawfish pie, etouffee, and crawfish bisque, and Robin's for homemade ice cream and other desserts. Robin's is also known as the first to develop a method of canning frozen crawfish. Visitors can purchase the same crawfish sold to Paul Prudhomme from the restaurant's hostess. I stopped in both restaurants and found spotless kitchens ringing with spoken French. Beyond the restaurants, the road becomes gravel. A turn to the right led me up along the levee where I saw a spectacular sunset dropping over the cypresses and low islands of the Atchafalaya Basin.

I took in the view from the bar at McGee's landing—also a good place to watch sunburned local "wildlife" gear up for the evening. Many boaters water ski or fish by day, using McGee's car park and boat-launching service.

CAJUN FUN & FOOD OVERLOOKING THE SWAMP

HOW TO GO:
I-10 past Baton Rouge and across the Atchafalaya Basin. Take the Ceceilia/Henderson exit and turn left toward Henderson. Left again on Hwy. 352. To get to the levee, go past Las's and Robin's Restaurant, cross the Henderson canal, and turn right by Pat's Restaurant. Follow the dirt road along the levee. Both McGee's and Basin Landing are clearly marked.

BEST TIME TO GO:
The swamp is most hospitable in spring and fall. Most of the levee's social activity centers around weekends.

From the levee near Henderson, the Atchafalaya Basin is a watery view as far as the eye can see. Fishermen, trappers, waterskiers, and tourists enjoy it by day, then meet for drinks and dinner atop the levee at McGee's landing in Henderson.

Robin's Restaurant

P.O. Box 542
Henderson, LA 70517
9:00 AM - 10:00 PM
Seven days
Ships frozen seafood entrees.
(318) 228-7594

McGee's Landing

1337 Henderson Levee Road
Henderson, LA 70517
Henderson Swamp tours, boat launch,
cafe, and bar.
(800) 445-6681

Basin Landing Houseboat Rentals

1219 Henderson Levee Road
Henderson, LA 70517
(318) 228-7880

At sundown they return to McGee's for bite-sized alligator snacks and Cajun dancing on the levee. McGee's hosts traditional—i.e. acoustical—French Cajun music Friday through Sunday. The Allemond family who runs McGee's established a boat launch on this site over fifty years ago. Now they operate swamp tours, a bait shop, weekend dance hall, cafe, and bar.

It's hard to watch all those returning boaters without yearning to explore the Basin. Next trip I plan to rent a houseboat at Basin Landing on the Levee near McGee's, so I can watch evening mist settle over the swamp away from the hustle and bustle.

Cajun Meat Markets

The last time I left New Orleans to visit family, I carried some unusual baggage: a large bundle of stuffed pork chops, tasso ham, and Cajun beef jerky. Airport security commented on the delicious aroma coming from my baggage and delighted family members put in orders for a repeat performance anytime.

My gifts came from meat markets in Cajun country where roadside signs announce fresh batches of boudin or jerky to the hungry traveller. Such specialty products can sometimes be found in New Orleans, but the quality of the country products convinced me to carry a cooler on every trip. As I comparison shopped, I learned that old time Cajuns swore by certain meat markets and ignored others. I set out to taste the difference and found flavors unique to Cajun country and freshness unavailable from a supermarket meat case. I learned that the best markets slaughter their own animals, cut meat to order for customers, and provide specialty products for holidays. They are usually family operations that have been in the business several generations, cooking with inherited recipes that reflect old-time Cajun tastes. Many serve hot plate lunches too, offering a limited choice of meals for $3 or $4 a plate.

While few of these markets would win awards for store decor, the owners are fun to talk to and the genuine article is worth the drive. Here are two of my favorites in the Cecelia/Henderson area:

Webster's Meat Market - known by the locals as Shookta's—but don't ask them how to spell it. "Shookta was my grandaddy's nickname, but I never saw it written down," said Teal Guidry. Guidry is the third generation to prepare stuffed pork chops, boudin, and cracklins for Cajun families in the Cecelia/Henderson area.

Many of Webster's customers ordered in French, but I didn't need an interpreter to know they were ordering what their fathers and grandfathers had ordered before them. Sunday's plate lunches are a community tradition too. Webster's sells out of their $4 hot lunches each Sunday, but you can call ahead to make sure you get one.

POCHE'S - The brass plaque outside says, "Landmarked for the preservation of our Cajun cuisine. Poche's is noted for the preparation of culinary food. It is from the Antoine Poche family ca. 1859 that originates the name of the village, Poche Bridge."

Poche's is a much bigger operation than most meat markets I visited, but the atmosphere is fun and the selection makes one-stop shopping for Cajun products easy. You can buy prepared roux, spice mixes, barbecue sauce, homemade sweet dough pies, pralines, and even fresh okra, in addition to all cuts of fresh and prepared meats. This is one of the few places that has specialty items like marinated turkey, beef tongue with garlic stuffing, tasso, and chaudin every day. Poche's serves between four- and seven-hundred chicken, pork, and sausage plate lunches each Sunday.

Taste the culture: Cajun butchers cut meat to specification, make boudin, andouille, and other local sausages, and smoke various delicacies on site.

WEBSTER'S MEAT MARKET
2685 Grand Point Road (Hwy. 347)
Between Cecelia and Henderson
(318) 667-6231
Closed Mondays
Tues - Fri. 7:00 AM - 5:00 PM
Sat. 7:00 AM - 4:00 PM
Sun. 7:00 AM - 12:00 PM

POCHE'S
3015-A Main Highway
Poche Bridge, LA 70517
(318) 332-2108

Sugarcane Festival & Museum

FARMERS SATISFYING AMERICA'S SWEET TOOTH

Drive anywhere in the twenty sugar producing parishes of Louisiana in September and you will see a glorious sight: oceans of gently undulating sugarcane tops begging for a haircut. It's a hectic time in the fields and in New Iberia, which hosts the Annual Sugarcane Festival in fall.

I visited sixth generation sugar farmer Mark Patout to learn more about his business. He took a break from his frantic September planting schedule to explain that sugarcane grows on a three-year cycle, beginning when a stalk of one year old "plant cane" is covered with soil. Cane that's planted this autumn, will be harvested next fall—and for two years after that —if hurricanes and freezes don't interfere.

"This is the busiest time of year for the sugarcane farmer. We're planting now and after that we'll be harvesting —up until Christmas some years. Farmers really don't have a chance to get out of the fields long enough to enjoy their own festival," said Patout.

Next year's crop of sugarcane springs from stalks of "plant cane" placed in the furrows of newly plowed fields during fall.

Even if farmers are in short supply at the festival, their families and everyone else around New Iberia participate, dressing as farmers on Farmer's Day and decorating everything with stalks of cane. Livestock sales, craft exhibits, sugar cookery demonstrations, boat parades, and fais-do-dos (Cajun dance parties) in honor of Sugarcane royalty add up to a full-blown country fair. King Sucrose and Queen Sugar host dozens of community events over the course of three days, honoring Louisiana's $300 million industry.

Patout recommended a visit to Le Beau Petit Musee in Jeanerette. The museum shows historic photos of sugarcane production and a videotape entitled *From Sugarcane to Sugar*.

Just outside Jeanerette, I saw an abandoned narrow-gauge railroad crossing Highway 90 near the intersection of Highway 85. Similar tracks were used by the the state's oldest family-owned sugar producer, M.A. Patout, to move cane from fields to mill. Looking to the south at that point, I saw the mill set among cane fields and a sign for Patoutville. The company was founded in 1829 by Pierre Simeon Patout. Mark Patout, one of two descendants still farming around Jeanerette, produces cane on 600 acres independent of the family company.

Back in Patout's field I spent a sticky morning watching a crew plant sugarcane. At 7:30 a.m. I stood with Patout, his partner, and 35 field hands at the end of a field of combed black earth. They'd been rained out the day before and were forced to start planting in a new area. Patout barked orders as we waited for wagons of "plant cane" to arrive. I mentally calculated the cost of 70 idle hands.

Finally four umbrellaed tractors hauling wagons of freshly cut cane fanned out across the field, followed closely by teams of men who laid three stalks of cane at regular intervals. By noon the teams had almost reached the far end of the field and the farmers were making plans for their lunch. I was scraping mud off my boots ready for the 140-mile drive back to New Orleans. It's not easy satisfying the American sweet tooth.

MAKING SUGAR OUT OF CANE

The process begins with harvesting the cane, then burning off the leaves while it is still in the fields. Autumn air carrying clouds of slightly sweet smelling smoke is a part of Louisiana that soon may be prohibited by the Environmental Protection Agency, but other signs of the sugarmaking process are everywhere in November and early December. In the old days, many plantations had their own mills connected to the fields by narrow-gauged railways. Today the cane is taken by truck to the nearest sugar house—a somewhat haphazard operation judging by the amount of cane spilled on the side of the road. Then the cane is ground to extract the juice, and the liquid is boiled and centrifuged until molasses has been separated from crystallized raw sugar.

When you pass a sugar house during the grinding, you will smell the syrup, and see clouds of steam and brown mountains of ground stems called bagasse. The rest of the operation is done in a refinery where raw sugar is washed and filtered to remove color and foreign matter.

Though modern sugar production is mechanized, you won't have to look far for signs of the old process. Many of the plantation homes have old sugar kettles incorporated into their landscaping schemes, reminiscent of the time when sugarcane juice was boiled over a fire and hand-stirred until it became molasses syrup.

HOW TO GO:

I-10 through Lafayette and U.S. 167 / 90 south to New Iberia. To reach Jeanerette take U.S. 90 east from New Iberia ten miles and turn north on either LA 85 or LA 318. Jeanerette is on the old River Road, Hwy. 182 between the two. For Sugarcane Festival parade and activity schedule call the Iberia Tourist Commission (318) 365-1540. Le Beau Petit Musee is open Mon. - Fri. from 8 AM to 5 PM. (318) 276-4408.

BEST TIME TO GO:

There's plenty of activity in the sugarcane fields from September through the harvest in December. Around Thanksgiving, cane is harvested and farmers burn off the leaves in the fields. Rural roads across Louisiana are lined with fallen cane and the smell of sugar processing fills the air.

Mills like this one south of Donaldsonville dot the cane-growing country of south Louisiana, transforming acres of sugarcane into tons of raw sugar.

Live Oak Gardens

CAJUN COUNTRY 1 to 3 HOURS

HOW TO GO:
U.S. 90 west to New
Iberia. Exit Hwy. 14
west. Drive six miles to
Rip Van Winkle Road.
Follow signs to Live Oak Gardens.
(318) 365-3332.

BEST TIME TO GO:
From mid-November through early
January the gardens are filled with
blooming camellias and sasanquas, and
the house is decorated for a Victorian
Christmas.

LIVE OAK GARDENS
5505 Rip Van Winkle Road
New Iberia, LA 70560
By admission: $$
9 AM - 5 PM open seven days.
(318) 365-3332

Speed bumps striped the road winding towards Live Oak Gardens, but they weren't needed to slow my car. I was already crawling, delighted by the endless row of live oaks that announced something extraordinary ahead. My destination was the salt dome on Jefferson Island, though I had no idea what that meant until the sight of a real hill at the end of the oak isle almost stopped my driving altogether. For someone who had been living below sea level in New Orleans, the prospect of 75 feet of elevation was dizzying. Could one breathe up there? Would there be a breeze?

Then I caught a glimpse of that hilltop house. If ever a house inspired mood, this was one. There's nothing sombre about this house. The architecture took cues from its setting: airy, triumphant, king of the hill. The cupola seemed to be flying, the Victorian carving looked like wedding cake, and the Steamboat Gothic and Moorish details were fantastic. It's easy to imagine its nineteenth-century builder, world famous actor Joseph Jefferson, on the wide porch at nightfall, spinning tales of pirate Jean Lafitte to a spellbound audience.

According to legend, Lafitte had a hideout on Jefferson Island. Treasure discovered beneath a giant live oak in the gardens a few years back adds weight to the legend.

The island is really a large cone of salt surrounded on three sides by Lake Peigneur. After Jefferson's era, a salt mine was established on one end of the island, its caverns extending beneath the lake. The lake leads into a bayou that no longer transports pirates to plunder, but shrimpers on their way to the Gulf.

Live Oak Gardens' entrance fee includes access to the house and extensive gardens, and an art museum. The gatekeeper said she hoped I'd have fun, and I think she meant it. Her attitude was reflected by every employee including the cafe cook who wouldn't let me leave without a taste of her fresh-baked brownies.

Crowning the salt dome at Live Oak Gardens, the home of actor Joseph Jefferson mixes Moorish, Steamboat Gothic, and other architectural styles.

I photographed black butterflies against red hibiscus and hummingbirds hovering over blue and pink water lilies—both species were migrating during my visit. Other visitors took the tours, worked their way through birdwatching checklists, and shopped for plants and garden ideas in the flowerbeds and the bookstore.

The museum on the property has exhibited travelling shows from the Smithsonian, and has a permanent collection of carved duck decoys. Like all facilities at Live Oak Gardens, the museum is wheelchair accessible.

Looking over the calm expanse of Lake Peigneur from the gardens, it was hard to imagine the bizzare industrial accident that occurred here in 1980. A video explains how an oil rig punctured the ceiling of the vast salt mine below the lake. Water rushed into the mine, creating a whirlpool that dragged in the drilling rig, eleven barges, tugboats, houses, 65 acres of land and all the water in the lake. The lake remained dry until the tide came in twelve hours later. Like everything else about Live Oak Gardens, this tale has a theatrical twist: The dollar toll of the accident was in the millions, but not one human life was lost.

Hibiscus and other warm weather plants fill Live Oak Gardens. Most of the garden's paths are wheelchair accessible, with plenty of benches for quiet meditation.

SHADOWS-ON-THE-TECHE

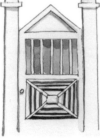

A few minutes drive from Live Oak Gardens in New Iberia, Shadows-on-the-Teche is another spacious antebellum home known for its hospitality to writers and artists. Cecil B. De Mille, H.L. Mencken, and Henry Miller are among those who enjoyed leisurely stays beneath the sweeping oaks.

Restored by William Weeks Hall, great-grandson of the original builder, Shadows is now owned by the National Trust for Historic Preservation. It is one of only 17 National Trust house museums in the United States, and it lives up to the honor. Mustard-colored walls, cinnamon-colored molding, faux marble, basket-weave brickwork and handcarved mahogany come together in a simple but elegant Classical Revival home overlooking Bayou Teche. Weeks Hall's patronage of the arts lives on in a regular series of art exhibits and lectures.

SHADOWS-ON-THE-TECHE

317 East Main Street
New Iberia, LA 70560
9 AM - 4:30 PM
By admission: $
Open seven days
(318) 369-6446

HOW TO GO:

From U.S. 90 exit onto LA 14 (Center Street) into downtown New Iberia. Shadows-on-the-Teche is located at the intersection of Center Street and Main Street (LA 182).

Acadian Cultural Center and Poupart's Bakery

ACADIAN & MODERN FRENCH CULTURE CO-EXIST IN LAFAYETTE

HOW TO GO:
I-10 west to Lafayette. South on U.S. 167 / 90 to Surrey Street. Follow Surrey to Fisher Road. Left on Fisher Road and right into the center's parking lot.

ACADIAN CULTURAL CENTER
P.O. Box 81081
Lafayette, LA 70598
Admission free.
(318) 232-0789

POUPART'S BAKERY
1902 Pinhook Road
Lafayette, LA 70508
(318) 232-7921

HOW TO GO:
In Lafayette take U.S 167 / 90 south to Pinhook Road. Right on Pinhook Road. Poupart's Bakery is on the right just beyond the intersection of Kaliste Saloom Road.

BEST TIME TO GO:
Early in the morning when locals stop in for coffee.

South Louisiana is full of immigrants' tales—and in Cajun country many of those stories are told in French two centuries after the first Acadians arrived in the country. In Lafayette, I got a quick course in French culture, simply by visiting the Acadian Cultural Center and the bakery of present day immigrant Francois Poupart.

The cultural center at Lafayette is the flagship of three interpretive sites operated by the National Park Service. Like the sites at Eunice and Thibodaux, the center's assemblage of photographs, time lines, and artifacts is open to the public with free admission. The most amusing display features audio recordings of Cajun jokes told in French and English. A park service film, *Echoes of Acadia*, runs on the hour. Though it's a bit overdramatic, the film gives more information about the Acadian migration than one could glean from days of exploring the surrounding countryside.

"Cajun country is very decentralized. That's why park service interpretation is so important. In fact the staffers at our information desk have a full-time job directing visitors to Cajun country happenings," said Unit Manager Dale Phillips. Unless you are fortunate enough to meet a Cajun family or stumble onto a community dance, this service is the best way to get the whole picture.

In the center's bookstore I found a zydeco music festival tape, a book on palmetto weaving, and a conical *capuchon* hat. From handmade dolls to musical spoons, the store features an excellent selection of local crafts.

I continued my shopping at Poupart's Bakery, just a ten minute drive from the center. The bakery's glass shelves overflowed with imaginatively decorated pastries. The Pouparts make everything from chocolate mice to classic, Parisian-style baguettes. They began the bakery in 1965 with just $50, selling their traditional French breads wholesale. Today their low fat bread is shipped to dozens of locations in Baton Rouge and Shreveport.

Master baker Francois Poupart and his family drive the French Loaf into the countryside on days off, looking for wild berries for their cakes.

Monsieur Poupart, who runs the business with his wife and son, enjoys talking. He explained his craft while sipping a cup of espresso at one of the bakery's cafe tables. A member of an ancient French guild system, Poupart apprenticed eight years before he earned the right to wear the earrings that are the trademark of *les compagnons*—France's master bakers. Monsieur Poupart still returns to his native France to teach his craft in *maison de compagnonnage* each year. Later, Poupart took me outside to see the "French Loaf," a handsome maroon and chrome bus which he takes around Louisiana collecting wild berries for his famous cream cakes.

Neither he nor his wife spoke English when they arrived in Louisiana in 1962, but it wasn't much of a problem since sixty percent of Lafayette's population still spoke French.

"We had to change many things. In France we use the sponge cake, but it is too dry for here. And of course po-boys are not French either. At first we only spoke French in the bakery. But today the customers speak it less and less," he said. Poupart has also picked up the *joie de vivre* of his Cajun neighbors. As he told the *Times of Acadiana* in a recent article: "Do you want to be a millionaire and work 24 hours a day? Or do you want to be happy?"

BONUS – ACADIAN VILLAGE AND VERMILLIONVILLE

Lafayette sports not one, but two replicas of Acadian settlements, Acadian Village and Vermillionville. The newer and more expensive version, Vermillionville is conveniently located next to the Acadian Cultural Center. Locals seem to prefer Acadian Village which is a project of the Lafayette Association for Retarded Citizens. Both are made up of old or replicated Cajun structures linked by paths and encircled by waterways. Vermillionville contains more copies of historic structures and it's more spread out— a disadvantage on hot days. However it also features Cajun food, demonstrations, artisans, and a dance pavilion with music in the afternoons. Though smaller, Acadian Village contains more authentic old structures, a museum devoted to Native Americans, and a large display about Dudley LeBlanc, purveyor of Hadacol, the once-famed patent medicine. Whichever settlement you choose, you can learn about such things as *traiteurs*, "jumping the broom," and *sabots*. I found friendly bilingual guides in both.

If your visit to Cajun country is brief, guides like these at Vermillionville provide a convenient way to experience Cajun culture.

ACADIAN VILLAGE
200 Greenleaf Drive
Lafayette, LA 70506
By admission: $
(318) 981-2364

HOW TO GO:
I-10 to the Ambassador Caffery exit. Drive south four miles to Ridge Road. Right on Ridge Road 1 1/2 miles, then left onto W. Broussard Road. Left on New Hope Road. Left on Greenleaf Drive.

VERMILLIONVILLE
1600 Surrey Street
Lafayette, LA
By admission: $$
(800) 99-BAYOU

HOW TO GO:
Follow directions to the Acadian Cultural Center, page 98. Vermillionville is next door.

BEST TIME TO GO:
Call ahead to find out about demonstrations, re-enactments, and tours. Both have self-guided tours as well.

Fred's Lounge
and Prairie Acadian Center

TWO-STEPPING INTO CAJUN CULTURE

HOW TO GO:
I-10 west through Lafayette to Hwy. 13. North on Hwy. 13 18 miles to Eunice. Continue on the same road 10 more miles to Mamou.

FRED'S LOUNGE
6th Street
Mamou, LA 70554
(318) 468-5411

PRAIRIE ACADIAN CULTURAL CENTER
3rd Street and Park Avenue
Eunice, LA 70535
(318) 457-8499
Admission free.

LIBERTY THEATER
2nd Street and Park Avenue
Eunice, LA 70535
(318) 457-7389
By admission: $

Itching to hear a Cajun dance band? A Saturday spent near Lafayette provides a sure cure. Begin the day at Fred's Lounge in Mamou, backtrack to Eunice for an afternoon at the Prairie Acadian Center, then cross the street for a live radio show at the Liberty Theater.

After driving two and one-half hours from New Orleans, it's not hard to find Fred's Lounge on the main street of Mamou—but it's rough to get there for the start of the party. I arrived around 11:30 one Saturday morning, and found that the crowd had been working up steam since 9 a.m. Not all parties in Cajun country start this early: the occasion at Fred's is a live morning radio show. You can hear it while driving to Mamou on KVPI radio—1250 AM. Fred's is open only on Saturday mornings and it's a good time that's been rolling for more than 40 years.

Some city people were dancing on the sidelines at Fred's, but most of the space was taken up by locals who looked as if they'd been born doing the Cajun two-step. Dance floor is too big a word for the two foot strip between the crowd and the roped off musicians, but no one seemed worried about having their toes squashed. Everyone clapped and stomped when a tanned, dark haired Cajun with flashing eyes repeatedly drag-

Stepping out on Saturday morning in Mamou, means a wild party at Fred's Lounge.

ged a waitress away from her duties to dance.

Fred's party ended at 1 p.m. and the bar emptied into the street with the twang and squeal of pedal steel and electric guitar ringing in our ears. I asked a couple from Mamou when they would go dancing next: "Tonight.

We'll go down the road and have some good fun. You want to know the way?"

Following their directions to Allen's Lakeview Park outside Eunice I found a clean, grassy campground next to a fishing lake that hosts a dance with local musicians every Saturday night. I couldn't stay for the dance, but I plan to go back for Mardi Gras when Allen's hosts a Courir du Mardi Gras—the customary horseback ride and party.

On the road to Eunice, I saw plenty of horses and cows grazing in knee high grasses, but it took a display at the Prairie Acadian Cultural Center to remind me that this was the home of the Cajun cowboy. The prairie areas west of Lafayette provided much of the beef for the south during the Civil War. Some of the hard-fighting black cowboys called Buffalo Soldiers who went west after the Civil War came from here too. I learned that the Buffalo Soldiers earned their name from Native Americans who were reminded of the buffalo's wooly hair and toughness.

Soon the scent of Cajun cooking drew me from the museum into the center's demonstration kitchen where a neighborhood woman was showing how to cook gumbo. She was one of over 25 area volunteers who make the center in Eunice a touchstone for Cajun culture with free demonstrations of quilting, music, weaving, and dance lessons. The enthusiasm of the volunteers makes visitors feel at home.

Across the street at the Liberty Theater a live radio and TV show features different area musicians, local recipes, and Cajun humor every Saturday night. There is no dance floor, but the audience has been known to dance in the aisles. It's a family style show at an early enough hour for a return drive to New Orleans.

BEST TIME TO GO:
Fred's is only open Saturday mornings from 9 AM until 1 PM. The Liberty Theater Cajun Grand Ol' Opry radio show is Saturday night from 6 - 8 PM. The Prairie Acadian Cultural Center across the street is open seven days a week. Interpretative programs, quilting, spinning, and cooking demonstrations are on Saturday at 3:00 PM. Sunday 2:00 PM the center holds a Cajun music jam session. Beginners are welcome.

Paris on the Bayou

PARIS ON THE BAYOU

HOW TO GO:
I-10 west to Breaux
Bridge. Hwy. 31 south to
St. Martinville.

PETIT PARIS
MUSEUM
St. Martin des Tours
Church Square
St. Martinville, LA
(318) 394-7334
9 AM to 5 PM, seven days a week.

The Presbytere of St. Martin de Tours Church in St. Martinville's town square, owes its style to the exiled French aristocrats who pioneered this part of rural Louisiana.

Refugees from the French Revolution, Napoleonic soldiers, and Longfellow's lovesick Evangeline figure into the tangle of myth and conjecture surrounding the historic Louisiana town of St. Martinville. Eager to find the truth about at least one early settler of St. Martinville, I set out with a friend whose French family name traces back to this small community on Bayou Teche.

"There's not much going on in that town," my friend cautioned before we began the two and one-half hour drive from New Orleans. I wasn't worried. How lively did it need to be for a visit to her family tomb and a check of the courthouse records?

The town square looked as it did 150 years ago. The church of St. Martin de Tour and the lovely formal buildings that surrounded it were painted in delicate creamy shades and set in carefully manicured gardens. A few French speaking tourists slipped out of the shadows of the church for a photograph. Otherwise the place was hot and deserted.

On one corner of the square, the Maison DuChamp, an 1870s house serving as St. Martinville's visitor center, displayed a painting of my friend's family coat of arms, sparse Victorian furnishings and a photographic display of a dozen buildings the town hopes to restore.

Under the nearby Evangeline Oak—made famous by Longfellow's poem about a tragic Cajun romance—brothers Ophe and Lennis Romero sat waiting to regale tourists with Evangeline related songs and stories. The two have become fixtures under the oak—and minor celebrities—since selling their cattle, horse, and rice farm in the 1960s.

"We've starred in three television commercials: two for cars and one for chicken. You just can't make it in farming these days," said one Romero.

Despite the heat, the brothers kept us entertained with photos and letters from France, a correspondence which they struggled to read using their Cajun French. Regretfully leaving the shade of the Evangeline Oak behind, we walked three steamy blocks to the Parish Court House.

In the cool of the courthouse archives, we saw signs reading "Ici On Parle Francais" (French Spoken Here). There, at shelves lined with records of succession from the 1700s, we leafed through pages of beautifully penned French until we found my friend's family name. In the 1750s the Chevalier of Louis XV was attached to Fort Attakapas, an outpost in Indian country which later became St.

Martinville. He and several other families kept aristocratic French culture alive, dancing minuets and inviting itinerant acting troupes to perform. This community of "Frenchmen from France" always stood apart from their Cajun neighbors.

Turning a fragile page of the records, I found the signatures of the Chevalier's sons on a document freeing a family slave. Decades later this French community attracted many Napoleonic soldiers who flooded Louisiana after Waterloo.

At the Petit Paris Museum, the extravagant lifestyle of St. Martinville's displaced nineteenth-century French is summed up in a charming legend. When two of Monsieur Charles Durand's daughters were to be married, he hit upon the idea of decorating the three-mile-long oak and pine alley in front of his house with spider webs. Large industrious spiders were brought in to make webs in the trees, and just before the wedding day, servants blew gold and silver dust into the gossamer canopy. The webbed wedding story became the theme of a 1984 Mardi Gras Pageant. The entire spider-covered court is represented by mannequins on the second floor of the Petit Paris Museum.

The statue of Evangeline in St. Martinville draws visitors familiar with Longfellow's epic poem about an Acadian woman searching for her lover.

DINING DETOUR – CAFÉ DES AMIS IN BREAUX BRIDGE

I went with two New Orleanians of discriminating palate to Café Des Amis in Breaux Bridge and they were pleasantly surprised. Owners Dickie and Cynthia Breaux have transformed an old dry goods store into an extraordinarily good restaurant.

Café Des Amis was cool, welcoming, and full of tempting aromas. We ordered corn bisque, grilled seafood salad, homemade root beer, and chicken fricassee, then browsed through their homey collection of books, crafts, and Breaux Bridge memorabilia while waiting to be served. The simple decorating scheme—dark wood floors, freshly painted white brick walls and stamped tin ceiling—displayed bright contemporary paintings and historical photos equally well.

Dickie Breaux, a politician turned restaurateur, went home to Breaux Bridge with the intention of recapturing the Cajun food of his youth. "I never ate any fried food as a kid," said Breaux. "The idea behind Cajun cooking was to stretch the food. We had such big families to feed. That's why there's rice in the sausage, sauces served over rice, and Cayenne pepper to extend the flavor."

Breaux incorporates contemporary cuisine, bucking tradition with an occasional white roux and grilled seafood bedded on lettuce. On the traditional side, he serves a wonderful dark chicken fricassee and pours ice cold homemade root beer from a seemingly bottomless pitcher.

CAFÉ DES AMIS
140 East Bridge Street
(318) 332-5273

HOW TO GO:
I-10 west to exit 109. South on Rees Street to Bridge Street. West on Bridge Street. Café Des Amis is on the left just across the bridge.

BEST TIME TO GO:
The cafe is open for breakfast, lunch, and dinner, but the hours change periodically. Call ahead to make sure.

Touring Alligator Country

EAT ALLIGATORS OR FEED THEM IN TERREBONNE PARISH

HOW TO GO:

Individual and small group visits to the home of Cajun trapper and alligator hunter Dovie Naquin can be arranged through:

A La Maison Cajun
French Tours
815 Funderburk Ave.
Houma, LA 70364
Bed and Breakfast Association of Houma-Terrebonne
(504) 868-9519 or (504) 879-3285

OR

Cajun Tours of Terrebonne
709 May Street
Houma, LA 70363
(504) 872-6157

S eptember is alligator season—and both alligator hunter Dovie Naquin and tour operator "Alligator Annie" Miller have competition in the normally quiet bayous of Terrebonne Parish. I visited both during the season's first week, learned about the hunters and the hunted, and took a closer look at life on the bayou.

Naquin, 80 years old, has been hunting alligators since he was a child. A native of Bayou Terrebonne, Naquin prefers speaking French to English. When he is not hunting or trapping, he entertains small tour groups in his raised cottage with stories and songs. When I arrived, Naquin was resting while his four sons stood shoulder-to-shoulder in a small porch skinning the nine alligators their father shot early that morning. "We tell him he does the easy part and we do the work" laughed Mark Naquin as the sound of his father's harmonica floated in the air above us.

In two days Naquin had captured 17 alligators. His sons stayed home from their jobs to help, rising with him at 4:30 a.m. and finishing the workday some 12 hours later. The alligator lines—baited steel hooks attached to 50-foot ropes—are laid late in the day and Naquin checks them at dawn, often travelling alone in pirogue and shooting any he has caught. At $42 per foot for a seven-foot alligator, Naquin's alligator hunting is a significant part of his livelihood. Still the season opener seems as much Naquin family reunion as it is an alligator hunt.

Dovie Naquin prefers to speak Cajun French when he tells of the annual alligator hunt near his property south of Houma.

Family members filled the small compound of houses where Naquin and his now-deceased wife raised seven children. Those who weren't busy with alligators entertained a steady stream of visitors. Others prepared the evening's meal of alligator piquant, crawfish etoufee, and smothered potatoes. Perfect hosts, the Naquin family shared their feast with a visiting script writer from California, a New Orleans artist and others, adding plates and glasses to the long, food-laden table on the screen porch. After dinner they danced the two-step, jig, and

Tour guide "Alligator Annie" feeds one of her pals during a swamp tour near Houma.

Cajun waltz, showing no sign of exhaustion from the day's work.

Surrounded by his happy family, Naquin recounted tense moments from the hunt. He spoke of his formidable opponents with respect and affection, referring to them by name. Last year he was flipped into the water by an alligator and lost his gun: "After I made it onto the shore, I said to him 'now we are even. You have my gun and I have my boat.' You heard a cat has nine lives? I used up three."

Swamp tour guide "Alligator Annie" Miller also addresses her alligators by name, calling them to a boatside dinner while her passengers observe.

"Baby, ba...by! Hurry up and get it...then go hide. You'll get shot if you stay here," she called to a large alligator that already had an old bullet wound. We saw plenty of evidence of the hunting season as we circled between open and protected waters, seeking Miller's alligator friends. Like giant mechanical wasps, men in air boats buzzed us then cut their engines and watched as we called large alligators. Miller eyed them in return saying, "They might have a friend with a tag and they'll tell where we are."

Miller brought out the largest alligators I have ever seen. Following her call, a little pair of eyes would appear way down the bayou and move steadily toward the boat, becoming a 12-foot monster. Then massive jaws snapped at the snack on the end of Miller's feeding pole. "Keep your hands in the boat and your feet off the rail," she reminded constantly.

As a guide, Miller had a bright and practical way of describing the swamps. She led us to an alligator line laid just outside the protected area, showed us great blue herons, and discussed the effects of agricultural chemicals on the swamps.

"I love the swamps and I love meeting the people," Miller said.

"ALLIGATOR ANNIE" MILLER'S TERREBONNE SWAMP AND MARSH TOURS

100 Alligator Lane
Houma, LA 70360
Fee: $$
(504) 879-3934

HOW TO GO:

Tours meet at Bayou Delight Restaurant eight miles west of Houma on U.S. 90 west.

BEST TIME TO GO:

September is open season for alligators, but Dovie Naquin accepts visitors year-round. Alligator Annie gives 2 1/2 to 3 hour tours between March 1 and November 1. Call for reservations.

SOUTHDOWN

Hwy. 311 at St. Charles Street
Houma, LA 70360
By admission: $
(504) 851-0154

HOW TO GO:

Cross the Crescent City Connection to
U.S. 90. Follow 90 south and west to
Houma. In Houma turn right on Hwy. 311
to St. Charles Street. Left on St. Charles,
follow the signs to Southdown.

BEST TIME TO GO:

Tours are on the hour 10 AM - 3 PM. Twice
a year the grounds around the old plantation house are filled with booths selling
antiques, handcrafted items, and Cajun
food. More than 300 vendors appear for
the biannual fund raiser, Southdown
Marketplace. Spring Marketplace is the
first Saturday in April. Fall Marketplace is
the first Saturday in November.

NEARBY – SOUTHDOWN PLANTATION IN HOUMA

When the Terrebonne Historical Society formed to save
Houma's Southdown Plantation from decay and ruin, members
had more in mind than the preservation of one old house. The
pink Victorian home had none of its original furnishings, so the
society made it a museum, with each room dedicated to a different chapter in the life of Terrebonne Parish.

Permanent exhibits range from Mardi Gras costumes to
Indian baskets—and include some unusual bedfellows—former Senator Allen J. Ellender's photo-filled Washington office
has been duplicated in one room, while the adjacent hall is
home to over 100 porcelain birds. It's all a bit overwhelming,
but a guided tour puts this profusion in context.

Honey-toned art glass windows with cane stalks, magnolia blossoms, and palmetto leaves frame the mansion's entry
hall, celebrating Southdown's agrarian heyday when 22,000
acres of sugarcane were processed in the plantation's own
mill. An early aerial photo shows the sugar mill towering above
Southdown 30 times the size of the house.

There were 88 sugar mills in Terrebonne Parish until
insects, disease, and the Great Depression destroyed the industry. The owners of Southdown helped develop a disease resis-
tant strain of sugarcane, but too late to keep them from finan-
cial ruin. Another display devoted to Terrebonne's industry and
transportation, told the story of Louisiana's Easter lily industry—big
around Houma in the 1940s and '50s until it too suffered from a disease.

The oil industry added another boom and bust saga to parish
history. "We're still recovering from the oil bust," commented the
museum guide. Then she pointed to a photo of a building that
housed both an undertaker and a gas station, "Thankfully we've
always known about diversification."

After the tour I took a closer look into a room dedicated to
local painter Charles Gilbert (1899-1970) and writer Dr. Thad St.
Martin. Gilbert painted moody Southern scenes with elastic looking figures reminiscent of Thomas Hart Benton and other regional
painters of the period. St. Martin was a medical doctor who min-
istered to the parish's remote, water-surrounded communities by
day and wrote novels about them at night. His 1936 book,
Madame Toussaint's Wedding Day described conditions in the
Cajun community with such frankness, authorities of the day dis-
couraged the reading of it. But I didn't have to look far to find a
copy. The book was re-issued by the Terrebonne Historical Society
and copies are available for sale in the museum's gift shop.

Wetlands Acadian Cultural Center and Bourgeois Meat Market

Thibodaux, Louisiana, is a working town—not a tourist stop—but visitors won't be disappointed. The Wetlands Acadian Culture Center is full of exhibits about local culture, a turn-of-the-century plantation village is nearby, and the town is home to a good Cajun meat market.

Located on Bayou LaFourche within a circle of sugar mills and cane plantations, Thibodaux is part college town and part agri-industrial. Driving down the town's main street, my view of St. Joseph's church spires was clouded by smoke from burning sugarcane, emphasizing the industry's continuing importance in the town's economy. But who could forget? Traffic piled up behind lumbering cane trucks and a ribbon of fallen cane lined the highways on both sides of the bayou.

Old fashioned sugarcane production is featured in the Wetlands Acadian Culture Center along with other Cajun occupations such as boat building, lumbering, hunting, trapping, and fishing. One of three National Park Service interpretive centers for Acadian culture, the Wetlands Acadian Culture Center conducted some of the first research into this area's Cajun and Creole culture. On weekends park rangers give interpretive talks: "Creoles of Color," "Boats of the Bayou," and "Acadian History and Settlement" are presented along with documentaries by master filmmaker Les Blank and others. Equally enjoyable are the museum's language and music rooms where recordings of Cajun French, Zydeco, and old-style Cajun waltz music play continuously.

My next stop, Bourgeois Meat Market, is a place to sample Cajun culture outside museum walls. There's nothing Cajuns like better than good food, and when it comes to meat, the spicier the better.

A delicious odor greeted me when I entered the market. "That's our beef jerky," said the man behind the counter. Beef jerky was an afterthought for the third generation of Bourgeois meat cutters. They made a tiny amount for a friend and one of their

FROM ANDOUILLE TO ZYDECO, CAJUN CULTURE THRIVES

HOW TO GO:

Hwy. 90 west past Des Allemands to Bayou Lafourche. Turn right or north on Hwy. 1. Follow Hwy. 1 into Thibodaux where it becomes West First. Right on St. Mary Street, the Wetlands Acadian Cultural Center is on your right.

WETLANDS ACADIAN CULTURAL CENTER

314 St. Mary Street,
Thibodaux, LA 70301
(504) 488-1375
Mon. 9 AM - 7 PM; Tues. - Thurs. 9 AM - 6 PM; Fri. - Sun. 9 AM - 5 PM
Weekend Interpretive Programs - 3 PM

The Thibodaux area has numerous drive-by-views such as Ardoyne, eight miles north of Houma on Highway 311.

BOURGEOIS MEAT MARKET

519 Schriever Hwy.
Thibodaux, LA 70301
(504) 447-7128
Mon. - Fri. 7 AM - 5:30 PM
Sat. 7 AM - 2 PM

HOW TO GO:

Follow St. Mary Street to Jackson Street. Right on Jackson Street, which then becomes Canal Blvd. In 3 1/2 miles take Hwy. 24 south. Bourgeois is on the left.

regular customers smelled it smoking and persuaded them to make 20 pounds for him each Monday. Today Bourgeois sells 700 pounds of jerky each week. According to owner Donald Bourgeois, Thibodaux area mothers shipped tons to soldiers serving in the Gulf War.

One of the few stores that operates its own slaughter house, Bourgeois Meat Market began in 1891. The key to their business is freshness: nothing is frozen, boudin is made daily, and they operate their own smoke house. They are one of the few to still make red boudin—a type of blood sausage that is strictly regulated by health officials. Crawfish boudin can be found at Bourgeois during crawfish season, from March through June. Their andouille sausage is the key ingredient to jambalaya and other local dishes. Bourgeois' exclusively retail business sells 2,000 pounds of boudin and 3,000 pounds of smoked sausage weekly. Apparently locals agree with my assessment of the family's work: "C'est bon!"

DOWN THE ROAD — LAUREL VALLEY VILLAGE

Looking for evocative Louisiana backdrops? Go where Hollywood does: *Angel Heart, Interview with the Vampire* and a recent rock video were all filmed outside Thibodaux at eerie, unpeopled Laurel Valley Village, the largest surviving sugar plantation in the United States. Though all but a restored general store is closed to the public, group tours of the complex can be arranged.

At the store, kittens tusseled on the porch and roosters strutted the yard. Inside, a cheerful volunteer showed off a mixture of museum artifacts and locally produced crafts. Old photos and objects from Laurel Valley sat beside handmade rag rugs and jewelry made from newspaper comic strips. Proceeds from sales support restoration of the historic site.

Deep in the cane fields behind the company store, the remains of a huge brick sugar mill suggests the size of the historic operation. The setting looks much as it did when Laurel Valley was the area's leading sugar producer. A matched set of 13 tin-roofed cabins curve around the compound's pond. Across the road, Creole "T" shaped houses and two-room shotgun houses sit beside fields of swaying cane that stretch to the horizon.

The 65 buildings that housed Laurel Valley's workers are tiny, unlit, and without running water. For most people, turn-of-the-century life was closer to camping than any modern notions of habitation.

Laurel Valley Plantation's complete set of turn-of-the-century housing for sugar workers outside Thibodaux, has attracted many Hollywood directors. With 72 buildings, it is the best preserved sugar plantation complex in the South.

"In those days people spent little time in a house. They ate, slept or procreated inside, but if the weather was good they often ate outside," said Dr. Paul Leslie, a history professor who leads tours through the complex.

Before the Civil War, Americans developed huge sugar plantations along Bayou Lafourche, displacing the original Acadian settlers and forcing them onto small ridges of dry land in the swamps. Laurel Valley's cane was first produced by slave labor, but that system and the original "great house" were destroyed in the Civil War. During Reconstruction many Acadians left the swamps to work for a newly industrialized sugarcane industry. By 1910 Laurel Valley had 450 employees—most of them white Acadians—and produced three million pounds of sugar.

"I always tell my students the Civil War not only set the black man free, but the Acadian as well," said Leslie.

Sugarcane is still produced by the Laurel Valley Corporation, whose majority stockholders are members of an Acadian family who have owned the plantation since the 1890s. Today cane is trucked out for processing, and a separate foundation, the Friends of Laurel Valley, has been set up to preserve the old industrial village.

Despite years of work, only a few buildings are completely restored, but Leslie's vivid descriptions bring Laurel Valley to life.

LAUREL VALLEY VILLAGE

LA Hwy. 308
Thibodaux, LA.
(504) 447-2902
Free admission.
Group tours by admission: $

HOW TO GO:

Alternate route to Laurel Valley and Thibodaux: U.S. 90 west and south past Des Allemands to Bayou Lafourche. Turn north on Hwy. 308 and follow the east bank of the bayou north to Thibodaux.

BEST TIME TO GO:

The store is open 11 AM - 4 PM on weekdays and 12 noon - 4 PM on weekends. Visitors who register at the store can drive into Laurel Valley Village and look at it from the road. A group of ten or more is required for tours. Call at least a week in advance.

Locally made crafts are sold throughout the year, but an especially large selection is available at the Christmas Open House, the first Sunday in December.

TRIPS OF ONE TO TWO HOURS
Mississippi

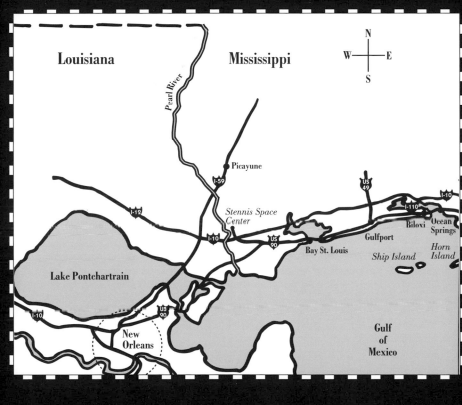

Louisiana

Mississippi

Pearl River

Picayune

I-59

Stennis Space Center

US 49

I-110

I-10

Biloxi

Ocean Springs

I-10

US 90

Gulfport

Horn Island

Bay St. Louis

Ship Island

I-12

Lake Pontchartrain

I-10

US 90

New Orleans

Gulf of Mexico

Beauvoir

LAST HOME OF CONFEDERATE PRESIDENT JEFFERSON DAVIS

MISSISSIPPI 1 to 2 HOURS

HOW TO GO:
I-10 east to Mississippi. Exit I-110 in Biloxi turning south toward the Gulf. Turn right (west) on I-90, Beauvoir will be on the right.

BEST TIMES TO GO:
Open 9 AM - 5 PM daily.
Avoid the weekend traffic on I-90.

BEAUVOIR
2244 Beach Boulevard
Biloxi, MS 39531
(601) 388-1313
By admission: $

Beauvoir, the last home of Confederate President Jefferson Davis, is a storehouse of Civil War artifacts and literature.

A traffic accident on the road ahead ruined our chance of reaching the ferry to Ship Island on time. Too far east of New Orleans to quit, our carload of daytrippers pressed on to the Mississippi shore. On a whim we pulled into the parking lot at Beauvoir, last home of Jefferson Davis, president of the Confederate States of America.

There was plenty of room to stretch at Beauvoir, and plenty to do as well. Some of our group visited the museum, with its darkened movie theater and glass display cases full of Confederate memorabilia. Others toured Jefferson Davis' house and some just walked the grounds. I went to the small pavilion overlooking the Gulf where Davis wrote his memoirs. Soft breezes and filtered light crossed the open sided room. It's said that after his imprisonment between 1865 and 1867, Davis had an aversion to being closed in —and this study was a perfect cure.

Thousands of war veterans made the pilgrimage to Beauvoir while Davis was alive, telling their stories or asking for his help. He seldom turned anyone away, making time and giving money—if he had it—to his former troops. Though his means were slim, Davis and his family lived well at Beauvoir by the good graces of Sarah Dorsey, a wealthy planter from Natchez. Initially she offered Beauvoir to Davis as a place to write his memoirs, but continued to extend her home to the family. Davis was buying Beauvoir when Dorsey died and left it to him. He lived there until his death in 1889.

One exhibit in the museum at Beauvoir is devoted to Davis' funeral in New Orleans. Old photos in "The Last Cause Remembered" show his casket lying in state and a three mile funeral procession from Jackson Square to Metairie cemetery.

Ten years after Davis' death, Beauvoir was purchased by the Sons of the Confederacy and used, according to the Davis family wishes, as a home for soldiers until 1957. Seven hundred seventy-one soldiers are buried in the Confederate

Cemetery on the property. After the soldier's home closed, the buildings were restored, a museum and library were added, and Beauvoir became the repository of a vast collection of Civil War memorabilia and literature.

The museum displays selected pieces from the Francis Lord collection of over 2,000 Civil War items focusing on soldiers' personal effects. The Jefferson Davis Memorial Library holds some 4,000 volumes on Civil War subjects.

I found Beauvoir's director, Keith Hardison, in the museum showing a child's Confederate uniform to visitors from Pennsylvania.

"Are you still fighting the war down here?" they asked.

"Yes, I think we are. We're conscious because the destruction was right here. Every Southerner can point to something that's been destroyed, and the fact that the South was in a colonial position until 30 or 40 years ago is a constant reminder," said Hardison, who has been a member of the Sons of Confederate Veterans since age 15 and can point to 10 relatives who were Confederate soldiers.

Hardison's pride in the South and Beauvoir were evident as he showed me the grounds: 57 acres fronting on the Gulf, embraced by swooping live oaks and laced with walking paths. In the Davis home 60 percent of the furnishings and all the frescoes are original. The compound of antebellum buildings exhibits the same spacious style it had when it was home to Davis.

"Those who forget the past have no future. We need this as a guidepost," Hardison said.

THE MAD POTTER OF BILOXI

He sported an 18-inch moustache, composed quirky double-exposed self portraits, saddled his children with names such as Zio and Ojo, and flew around the streets of Biloxi on a bicycle with long hair streaming behind. But when 8,000 pieces of George Ohr's turn-of-the-century pottery were rediscovered in 1968 the face of American art pottery changed. Unheralded in his lifetime, except for his eccentric behavior, Ohr's facility with paper thin clay, extraordinary glazes and "tortured" forms is unrivaled. In 1994 Biloxi's Gulf Coast branch of the Mississippi Museum of Art became the George E. Ohr Arts and Cultural Center and built a new gallery to house 150 pieces of Ohr's work. A potter's wheel and interactive displays for children are included.

GEORGE E. OHR ARTS AND CULTURAL CENTER
136 George Ohr Street
Biloxi, MS 39530
Free admission.
Tues - Sat. 10 AM - 5 PM
Sun. 1 - 5 PM
(601) 374-5547

HOW TO GO:
East of Beauvoir on U.S. 90, the cultural center is adjacent to the Biloxi Public Library. Past I-110, turn left off U.S. 90 onto George E. Ohr Street. The cultural center is on the right.

BEST TIMES TO GO:
Hours are subject to change. The museum is not crowded, but U.S. 90 is very crowded on the weekends.

Characterized by paper thin walls, twisted forms, and unusual glazes, 8,000 pieces of George Ohr's pottery once lay forgotten in Biloxi, Mississippi. Today individual pieces sell for what a New York collector paid for the lot in 1973.

J.L. Scott Marine Education Center and Aquarium

HOW TO GO:
I-10 east to Mississippi. Exit 46 to I-110 (D'Iberville) south in Biloxi and drive south to Hwy. 90. East on 90 two miles. The center is on the right at the foot of the bridge that connects Biloxi and Ocean Springs.

J.L. SCOTT MARINE EDUCATION CENTER AND AQUARIUM
115 Beach Blvd. (U.S. Hwy. 90)
Biloxi, Mississippi 39530
(601) 374-5550
Mon. - Sat. 9 AM - 4 PM
By admission: $

I f you take your children to the J.L. Scott Marine Education Center and Aquarium in Biloxi, you're likely to hear a complaint the next time you are tempted to litter.

When I visited the center I saw a fish whose head and fins were deformed by a discarded plastic six-pack ring and another that had been caught in a rubber gasket. The maimed fish adapted and were swimming in the center's aquariums with hundreds of other species, but only because researchers nursed them back to health.

There are 40 aquariums and an auditorium with continuously running marine-science documentaries in the modern education center located at the end of Biloxi's string of waterfront casinos. The centerpiece is a 42,000 gallon tank filled with sharks, turtles, eels, and fish from the Gulf of Mexico. Another tank unveils nocturnal species.

The center is a lively place, filled with attractive displays of sea shells from around the world, bubbling aquariums, and the laughter of delighted children playing in the "hands-in, touch tank." While I kept a distance from the hermit and horseshoe crabs, several small children sent experimental waves over the starfish in the bottom of the tank. Other kids peered wide-eyed through a glass tank at non-poisonous snakes. A well-designed self-guided tour makes this place user friendly for adults and children, but the fascinating sight of sharks swimming above eye level and turtles as big as jet-skis requires little explanation.

The education center is a spin-off of the Gulf Coast Research Laboratory in Ocean Springs. "This place got started because we had so many requests for information," said Center Director Dr. Sharon Walker. Educational programs for the public use the Biloxi facility as a base for field trips and specimen gathering. Throughout the summer there are four-day Marine Discovery Sea Camps for kids and barrier island based mini-camps for teachers.

"We try to teach kids because their environmental ethic is so good and when they grow up to be voters, they will make the right deci-

Biloxi's Marine Education Center takes the mystery out of the Gulf with giant aquariums and hands-on displays.

sions," said Walker. "You can show them the impact of marine litter. It's either entanglement or ingestion. Sea turtles—all eight species are endangered—think plastic bags are jellyfish, their favorite food. When they ingest the plastic they become impacted. Their intestines are pierced by the corners of the plastic bags. I tell kids that if Christopher Columbus had plastic and threw it off his ship in 1492, it would just be starting to disintegrate today."

After touring the education center, Walker and I stood outside overlooking the newly built and frantically busy casino parking lots next door. "All that used to be green," Walker gestured to a huge black-topped parking lot with new landscaping. "Those shrubs aren't native and they will not do as well. People need to understand the trade-offs. I wouldn't want those people to lose their jobs, but some animals needed that beach to nest."

MARITIME AND SEAFOOD INDUSTRY MUSEUM

There's history behind your heaping seafood platter and you can find it at the Maritime and Seafood Industry Museum in Biloxi, Mississippi.

Today glass-fronted casinos conceal a waterfront that once had rows of seafood canneries and a harbor filled with billowing white sails. When Hurricane Camille came ashore in 1969, she wiped out dozens of factories, clearing the land where most of the casinos now stand.

At the turn of the century there were more than 40 seafood factories in the town, and Biloxi was so central to the industry that one style of fishing vessel bears the town's name. Biloxi schooners, called "white-winged queens" for their full, white sails, have long since been replaced by boats with engines.

These days trawls are used in place of hand-drawn seines, and refrigeration along with air freight have put a dent in the canning industry. But you can still get a sense of Biloxi's industrial triumph by visiting the museum or taking a trip on its excursion vessel, a Biloxi Schooner replica.

On a recent Gulf coast drive I took a break from the traffic along the coastal highway, and spent a quiet hour in the museum. Displays tracing the development of the "Seafood Capital of the World" began with some early fishermen: Biloxi Indians whose ancient pottery shards were covered with sea life patterns that reminded me of the work of twentieth-century Ocean Springs artist Walter Anderson.

Throughout the museum, oyster tongs, shrimpers' boots, and other tools of the trade provided artful three dimension relief from painstakingly prepared charts and historic photos. These displays

Once typical tools on Biloxi's waterfront, this pilot's ladder and ice chipper are preserved along with historic harbor views, cannery labels, and child labor documents at the Seafood Industry Museum.

MARITIME AND SEAFOOD INDUSTRY MUSEUM

P.O. Box 1907
Biloxi, MS 39533
(601) 435-6320
By admission: $

The Biloxi schooner, the Glenn L. Swetman is available for 2 1/2 hour sails as well as half- and full-day charters. Call for reservations.

HOW TO GO:

From the intersection of I-110 and I-90 in Biloxi drive east along the waterfront. Turn left before the bridge and follow signs to the museum.

BEST TIME TO GO:

Open Mon. through Sat. 9 AM - 5 PM, but I like to go on Tuesdays or Thursdays when the farmer's market is open next door.

On Tuesdays and Thursdays, a full-scale farmer's market is held in an open area next to the museum. My friends and I came away with snapdragons, pumpkins, honey, field peas, Indian corn, green beans, and tomatoes—all homegrown in Mississippi. There were also live rabbits, ducks, and turkeys for sale.

could be read at a glance or enjoyed at leisure. Next to samples of gill nets, trammel nets, and drag seines were pictures of net weavers working with both toes and fingers. Half models, blueprints, and photographs delineated the differences between cat boats, trawlers, and other vessels that plied the Gulf waters. The designers of this museum thought of every visitor: Kids can take rubbings from bas relief images of sea life; shoppers will find a museum store with maritime books, posters, jewelry, and oversized postcards made from old cannery labels.

Elsewhere I found photographs of Biloxi factory workers by documentarist Lewis W. Hine. Taken in 1913 while Hine was staff photographer for the National Child Labor committee, the photos reveal the condition of children who labored 11 hour days in factories picking crabs or cleaning shrimp.

Another documentary exhibit was devoted to hurricanes. There have been 30 such storms in Biloxi's history, but most locals still speak with awe of the 1969 devastations of Hurricane Camille. An old-fashioned docu-drama plays continuously in the exhibit. Its vivid scenes of palms bent horizontal and howling hurricane winds came to my mind again on the museum's front lawn. I watched casino traffic rush past and realized I stood where a hurricane had once destroyed the town's livelihood, and could easily do it again.

Horn Island

Among the Gulf coast's best kept secrets are National Park Service wilderness areas such as Petit Bois and Horn Island. Both can be reached by charter boat, and may be used for wilderness camping where you must carry-in all water, food, and shelter and pack-out all traces of your stay on the island.

I took the ten-mile offshore trip to Horn Island to see where Ocean Springs artist Walter Anderson retreated for weeks of uninterrupted drawing and painting. Anderson rowed all day to reach the island. I made it in one-half hour by motor boat and discovered a place that still had the pristine beauty that drew Anderson decades ago. The dunes were higher than I expected and topped with majestic twisted pines. An unpeopled white sand beach stretched as far as I could see in either direction and the interior of the island was thick with tangled vegetation. The only sounds were the wind whistling through the pine trees, the waves and the cries of dolphins off-shore. Sprawling osprey nests crowned the tallest trees and alligator paths looked like pine needle bobsled chutes through the thicket. On the beach I saw horseshoe crabs, ghost crabs, countless shells, and higher up where the sand was dry, an "S" shaped snake trail. No wonder Anderson rowed all day long to reach Horn Island—it is a naturalist's paradise.

Because the Gulf islands are so isolated, the park service has used them to reestablish endangered populations of the Bald Eagle, Perdido Key Beach Mouse, Brown Pelican, and Red Wolf species. Horn Island is a release site for young eagles and a breeding compound for a pair of Red Wolves. When the program began two years ago, only 88 Red Wolves were known to exist. Seven wolf pups were born on the island, then transferred back to their natural range land in the Carolinas. Drifting away from my companions, I was the first to spot fresh Red Wolf tracks in the sand. People seldom see the shy creatures, and that is why fresh tracks were so exciting. The male wolf must have been on the beach when we arrived.

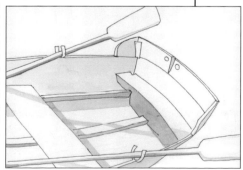

NATURE SANCTUARY ON DESERT ISLE

HOW TO GO TO HORN ISLAND:

King Marine Service
120 Sunshine Dr.
Ocean Springs, MS 39564
(601) 875-9491

Round trip camping service. Minimum two persons. Wilderness tours offered.

Naturalist Charter, Inc.
505 Front Beach Dr.
Ocean Springs, MS 39564
(601) 875-1413

Custom eco-tours of rivers, bird refuges, and islands.

Biloxi Seafood Industry Museum
P.O. Box 1907
Biloxi, MS 39533
(601) 435-6320
(Replica Biloxi schooner sailing vessel.)

Tours available for groups of 20. Half-day and full-day sails available.

BEST TIME TO GO:

Spring and fall provide the most relief from heat and insects.

*Note: In Spring 1996, East Ship Island will open for wilderness camping. Reserve through Pan Isles (601) 875-9057.

Artist Walter Anderson rowed all day to reach his solitary retreat on Horn Island. I made it in 30 minutes, but still found an undisturbed wilderness.

Horn Island forms a barrier between the Gulf of Mexico and the Mississippi Sound.

Wolves aren't indigenous to Horn Island, but large numbers of rabbits are. When the park service released the wolves, they monitored the effects on the rabbit population. To their surprise the average age of rabbits decreased but not the overall numbers. Apparently the wolves ate the older rabbits, leaving more food and good breeding conditions for the younger ones.

One narrow corridor within Horn Island's 3,700 acres is used by the park service. Two rangers live on the island in a modest government green house behind a fanciful driftwood sign that says, "Horn Hilton." I asked district ranger Mark Lewis about the two years he lived on the island. "Not a day passed without finding some sort of surprise on beach patrol. One day it was a half dozen oranges that drifted in from who knows where. They last forever bobbing around in the water, so there was breakfast. Another morning I spotted fresh footprints coming straight out of the sea and into the woods. I looked around all morning then found this 18-year-old kid, who jumped off a shrimp boat two miles out and swam to what he thought was the mainland. He didn't know where he was—he just knew he didn't like shrimping!"

Everything on Horn Island is protected, from the water mocassins to the sea oats. The park service's dual mandate—to provide recreational areas and to protect natural resources—conflict in fragile areas like the barrier islands. That is why visits to wilderness areas are not widely promoted. Access to Horn Island is via three park service approved charters listed on page 117. Trips are occasionally sponsored by the Audubon Society and the Nature Conservancy.

DAVIS BAYOU

Gulf Islands National Seashore
3500 Park Road
Ocean Springs, MS 39565
(601) 875-0821
Free admission.

HOW TO GO:

The entrance to Davis Bayou is off Hwy. 90 east in Ocean Springs.

GULF ISLANDS NATIONAL SEASHORE AT DAVIS BAYOU

Ship Island and Horn Island are administered by the Gulf Islands National Seashore based at Davis Bayou in Ocean Springs, Mississippi. Set in 400 acres of marshland adjacent to the Gulf, Davis Bayou has campgrounds, picnic areas, a boat ramp, nature trail, and fishing pier. The visitor center shows films describing the eco-system operating on the barrier islands and in the coastal marshes. There is also a display of shore and marshland wildlife, beautifully carved out of wood. A few times per week in summer, rangers give johnboat tours of the marshes. Call for times.

Ship Island Excursions

t was nearly 100 degrees the day I ferried to Ship Island off the Mississippi coast. I scarcely ventured beyond the circle of shade cast by my beach umbrella, but still acquired a decent case of heatstroke by mid afternoon. White sand, clear blue water, and a beach full of happy bathers danced before my eyes like a mirage. Children's laughter mixed with the cries of laughing gulls from far away.

Maybe it was a mirage. The closest white sand, blue water beach was supposed to be in Florida, but even with heatstroke I remembered I was in Mississippi, where beaches are supposed to be lapped by brown water. The 12-mile trip to West Ship Island, part of the Gulf Islands National Seashore, takes you across the mud-colored Mississippi Sound to the barrier islands—thin strips of sand that divide the Sound from the clear waters of the Gulf of Mexico.

The nearest ferry to Ship Island is in Gulfport, an hour and a half drive from New Orleans. Then, it's a 55-minute ferry ride to the Gulf Island National Seashore recreation site on West Ship Island. A second ferry departs from Biloxi. Between the two, this barrier island preserve gets a few hundred visitors daily during the season. Everyone must leave at night, and the beach, showers, and snack bar are returned to picture-perfect cleanliness by a staff of National Park service employees.

Excess baggage and glass bottles are best left behind on this island trip. The walk from the ferry dock on the Sound to the beach on the Gulf side of the island takes 15 minutes—far enough to require comfortable footwear and a light load. Food is for sale on the ferry and the island. Beach chair and umbrella rentals are available on the beach.

A wooden boardwalk crosses the island, linking landscape suited for alligators and water mocassins, to a sandy environment full of sea birds and scuttling crabs. Along the way, morning glories and palmettos bend in the steady sea breeze.

On the Gulf side I made a hot-footed dash across sand dunes to clear water that turned cool at shoulder depth. Like most visitors I wasn't dressed for exploring the marshy interior of the island, but at low tide, I walked the beach, dodging stranded jellyfish and watching hermit crabs drag their shells across the wet sand.

Most visitors frolicked on the swimming beach, fished in the surf, or toured Fort Massa-

ISLAND BEACHES DRAW BLUE WATER BATHERS AND NATURALISTS

HOW TO GO:
From Gulfport: I-10 east to Mississippi. U.S. 49 south to Gulfport. The Ship Island ferry is at the Gulfport Yacht Harbor near the intersection of U.S. 90 and U.S. 49. (Turn beneath the sign for Marine Life.) From Biloxi: I-10 to I-110 south. The terminal is at the intersection of I-110 and U.S. 90 next to Buena Vista Beach Club Inn.

BEST TIME TO GO:
Ship Island ferries run from March to October. Unless you are a hardy sun-worshiper, take the trip in spring or fall.

PAN ISLES, INC.
P.O. Box 1467
Gulfport, MS 39502
(601) 864-1014
Ferry times vary seasonally.
Call for schedule.
Ferry ticket: $$$

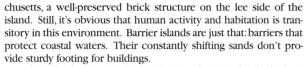

chusetts, a well-preserved brick structure on the lee side of the island. Still, it's obvious that human activity and habitation is transitory in this environment. Barrier islands are just that: barriers that protect coastal waters. Their constantly shifting sands don't provide sturdy footing for buildings.

Ship Island was completely submerged except for the highest rooms in Fort Massachusetts during hurricanes in 1947 and 1969. The few inhabitants who took shelter in the fort spent a miserable night fending off the island's other occupants: snakes, rats, and alligators. Such storms, along with prevailing currents, actually move the island in a westerly direction at a speed of three and a half miles every hundred years. In 1960, local residents, fearing that Ship Island was leaving Fort Massachusetts behind, spearheaded efforts to reinforce it with riprap from Highway 90.

"Horseshoe crabs are not crabs at all. They're arachnids that have been around since the dinosaur age," a Park Ranger informed me. Natural history lessons and beach walks are part of the package offered by the Park Service to Ship Island visitors.

I took the tour of Fort Massachussetts, where winding interior stairwells and breezes through gun ports provided cool contrast to the beach. Well-preserved brick walls and archways tell the story of fort construction at the time of the Civil War. Lower, pale-colored bricks came from St. Joe Brickworks in Slidell, while the darker red bricks above them were brought in from Boston by occupying Union soldiers. The reappearance of pale Slidell bricks at the top announce Reconstruction.

Park service rangers offer special weekend tours that range from naturalist walks to Civil War history recounted in period costumes. "Soldier Life" and the "Civil War Program" add period costumes and details to the basic fort tour. "Island Treasures" and "Beach Walk" focus on Ship Islands plant and animal life.

At the ranger station I found a natural history lesson in progress, with props that included a loggerhead sea turtle skull, a four-legged starfish with a regenerating stump, dolphin vertebrae, and horseshoe crab shells—all specimens gathered by rangers during their daily rounds. "Visitors are not permitted to injure any shrub or tree, pick the sea oats, or collect the wildlife," states park literature.

Yet despite its fragility, the environment on a barrier island is strangely hostile to humans: sun, wind, and insects are unmerciful. Fresh water is a constant concern. Clad in long pants and sensible hats and shoes, the park rangers are schooled in first aid for heatstroke and sunburn.

Most visitors, myself included, were the color of the fort's bricks by mid afternoon and exhausted by sun and swimming. Island employees gathered up stragglers and herded us back to the mainland, where we traded our desert island daydreams for cars and other trappings of city life. One thing was certainly not a mirage: Everyone looked happier and more relaxed after a day at the beach.

SHIP ISLAND'S INLAND SHORE

Most visitors to Mississippi's Ship Island haul coolers and march directly across the island to the white sand and blue water of the Gulf. But the inland side of this shifting barrier island has allure for fly fishermen and those dreaming of deserted beaches.

The sand on the inland beach is more firm than the Gulf side, and the wind is more gentle. When the tide comes in and fish are active, the big flats and light surf of the inland side make wading and casting a fly rod easier. The rocks near the old lighthouse and an old barge wreck near the fort are two places cited by local fly fisherman as excellent for sea trout and red drum fishing. They recommend heavy rods—a seven or eight weight—and some top water poppers in bright colors: red and white, hot pink, and chartreuse. Fishing licenses, tide charts, and regulations are available on the island.

Rangers encourage fishermen to release their catch because the island's waters hold many small fish that need time to grow.

The less-crowded inland shore of Ship Island, with Fort Massachusetts and the ferry landing in the distance.

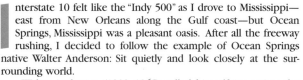

Walter Anderson Museum

ECCENTRIC GULF COAST ARTIST CELEBRATED IN FIRST-RATE MUSEUM

HOW TO GO:

I-10 east past Biloxi to Hwy. 609. South to Ocean Springs. The Walter Anderson Museum of Art is located at 510 Washington Avenue. (601) 872-3164. Check at the museum for directions to Shearwater Pottery. (601) 875-7320

BEST TIMES TO GO:

Weekdays—but only to avoid freeway and beach traffic on the way.

WALTER ANDERSON MUSEUM OF ART

510 Washington Ave.
Ocean Springs, MS 39564
By admission: $
Tues. - Sat. 10 AM - 5 PM
Sun. 1 - 5 PM

SHEARWATER POTTERY

102 Shearwater Drive
P.O. Box 737
Ocean Springs, MS 39564
(601) 875-7320
Mon. - Sat. 9 AM - 5:30 PM

Interstate 10 felt like the "Indy 500" as I drove to Mississippi—east from New Orleans along the Gulf coast—but Ocean Springs, Mississippi was a pleasant oasis. After all the freeway rushing, I decided to follow the example of Ocean Springs native Walter Anderson: Sit quietly and look closely at the surrounding world.

Walter Anderson (1903–1965) called himself "an artist who prefers nature to art." He produced exceptionally energetic drawings of birds, plants, and other wildlife, much of it in watercolor on typing paper. He lived and worked in the town when he wasn't taking lengthy island retreats, something he did more often as he grew older. I don't know what intrigued me more: the wallpaper-like repetition of his drawing style; the stories I'd heard of his eccentricities; or the idea of disappearing to an island with watercolors and a large supply of typing paper. Anyway I was eager to visit the Walter Anderson Museum which turned out to be better than I expected.

It is a modern building, comfortable in size, well-lit and air-conditioned. Part of the museum is a tiny shrine-like painted room that was discovered in Anderson's house after his death. Another very large room, its walls covered with pictures of diving eagles and blossoming plants, is still a functioning civic center for the Ocean Springs community. A small theatre continuously shows a documentary film about the artist. Much of the rest of this professionally run museum houses the artist's voluminous body of nature renderings. I browsed around the cool, quiet galleries, looked at the toys he made and the boat he rowed out to Horn Island, then headed for the beach.

The tiny harbor with its jumble of small craft was as picturesque as any New England calendar photo. Barrier islands anchored just below the horizon appeared to be vibrating in the heat, and people meandered across the white sand beaches. On the pier I talked to other people who seemed to take Anderson's approach to heart. They were spending the after-

My trips to Ocean Springs always include a shopping stop at Shearwater Pottery, an Anderson family business. Many historic designs are still produced, including this figurine by Walter Anderson.

noon sitting in the shade, looking out to sea. They weren't eating, drinking, or fishing—just sitting and looking. They had never been to the museum, but remembered Walter Anderson as an offbeat sort who looked at nature a lot.

There are plenty of others who remember Walter Anderson. The rest of the Anderson family runs the Shearwater Pottery factory, located on a shady, pine-covered point of land not far from the harbor. The showroom is open to visitors, and I found that it was fun to figure out which pieces were designed by Walter Anderson or created by his brother or son. The array of lamps, platters, and small figurines were tempting. During regular business hours, visitors can watch the pottery being produced in the factory down the road from the showroom.

Given a choice, I'd save a visit to Ocean Springs for a weekday. It's a peaceful sort of place that doesn't bear weekend crowds well. Despite this, Ocean Springs is a beautiful spot and the Walter Anderson museum alone is well worth the trip.

REALIZATIONS

In 1985 the Anderson family opened Realizations, Ltd.: the Walter Anderson Shop. There they use the late artist's linoleum block designs to embellish everything from pot holders to women's dresses. Anderson created the blockprints between 1945 and 1949 as "public" art, or art—at a dollar a foot—that anyone could afford. The prices aren't that low anymore, but his wonderful, linear designs hold up well in almost any application. Realizations is located in the old Louisville and Nashville train depot at the Washington Avenue railroad crossing.

REALIZATIONS, LTD.
THE WALTER ANDERSON SHOP
1000 Washington Ave.
Ocean Springs, MS 39564
  (601) 875-0503

Everything artist Walter Anderson drew, painted, or sculpted came alive. Here, a toy bull Anderson made for his children shows some of his spirit.

Crosby Arboretum

PINES TO PALMETTOS:
MISSISSIPPI LANDSCAPE
INTERPRETED AT
NATURE PRESERVE

HOW TO GO:
I-10 east to Hwy. 59 N.
Just after entering
Mississippi, exit 4 to the
right and follow signs to
the Crosby Arboretum.

WHEN TO GO:
Weekend programs, guided tours, and
field trips are offered monthly. Call for a
schedule.

CROSBY ARBORETUM
1986 Ridge Road
Picayune, MS 39466
Wed. - Sun. 10AM - 5 PM
By admission: $
(601) 799-2311

I toured Pinecote, Crosby Arboretum's interpretive center in Picayune, Mississippi, with a group of aspiring 13-year-old environmentalists. They examined fish-filled pools and memorized orchid species as they trained for camp counselor positions.

"This training will look good on my resume," said one boy as we paused beneath a spreading red maple to look across a dark mirrored pool.

"Do you think about resumes at your age?" I asked.

"Well really it's my mother who thinks I need to work on my resume. I just like nature," he said. The junior counselors chattered happily between brief lessons on oxygen producing algae, insect eating plants, and savannas regenerated by fire.

"There are more species per square mile in the Western Mississippi and Eastern Louisiana wetland environment than any other area of the United States," said their guide, arboretum director Ed Blake.

Founded in 1979, the Crosby arboretum is actually a network of preserves designed to conserve habitat indigenous to the Pearl River watershed. It consists of eight separate sites that range from a quaking bog to an upland long leafpine forest. The sites are used by area schools for environmental research and some are so fragile that public access is limited. Pinecote, however, was designed to present miniature exhibits of habitat to the public.

Once a strawberry farm, Pinecote was modified to add wetlands and woodlands to an existing slash pine savanna. "There were no lakes here before we put them here. It's been very interesting to watch the plant and animal life evolve—many of the species we have in the arboretum appeared in a very natural way. Take fish for example: fish eggs were brought on the feet of the egrets who came here hoping to feed. Now the fish are so numerous the arboretum opens for a fishing day once a year. Last year one angler came away with a four-and-a-half pound bass," said Blake.

In 1986 the award winning Pinecote pavilion was built and received rave reviews in the architectural community. Designed by Faye Jones, student of famed American architect Frank Lloyd Wright, the pavilion is used for open-air dinners, concerts, and lectures. Despite the rich plant and animal life, Blake

Pinecote Pavilion won national awards for a design that mirrors the forms, and frames the landscape of Crosby Arboretum.

considers Pinecote essentially urban site. New Orleans is only 45 miles away, and distant highway noise could be heard throughout the preserve. Rather than ignore the noise, Blake used it to underscore the complexity of our environmental problems: "The question is this," said Blake, "If you need to protect your feet, do you pave the earth in leather or make shoes? I guess we need to learn to make quieter machines."

The Crosby Arboretum is a user friendly environment: wheelchair accessible ramps and bathrooms, comfortable meandering walking paths, and benches designed to easily get next to the water and really look. The visitor center and gift shop highlights local crafts.

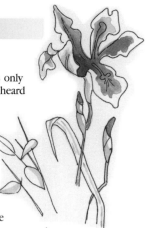

Wild Iris at Crosby Arboretum.

STENNIS SPACE CENTER

Trace the Pearl River south on a Mississippi map and you will find a huge, seemingly blank, area marked "NASA Test Site." The Stennis Space Center was built in 1963 to test NASA's rocket propulsion systems.

It takes a visit to the Stennis Space Center to grasp the space program's impact on the Gulf coast. The base covers 200 square miles of slash pine forest and wetlands adjacent to the Pearl River. Families in five small towns signed over land that had been theirs since the days of Jean Lafitte to what was the country's second largest construction project. More than 10,000 jobs were created by the project.

You can reach Stennis Space Center via the first exit off I-10 going east into Mississippi. At the gate a guard checks all who enter the base, and then you follow several miles of pristine, forest-lined highway to the visitor center. On first glance you would never guess that 4,000 employees work in the complex. The road crosses canal locks and passes a city-sized water tower, but much of the view consists of an exceptionally large unbroken stand of trees.

Eventually three enormous steel and concrete rocket test stands come into view. One stands 290 feet tall and was for a time the tallest structure in Mississippi. Seven-and-a-half miles of canals allow barges to deliver rocket engines to the test stands and a 66 million gallon reservoir provides water to cool the flame buckets that surround the engine casings. During tests the trees form an acoustical buffer for the roar of rocket engines, but on nights with cloud cover the rockets can be heard across the Louisiana line in Slidell.

Visitors can tour the complex by bus and see an engine test, if one is scheduled for the day. Tests are more dramatic than launches, since the rocket disappears into outer space moments after the

JOHN C. STENNIS SPACE CENTER

Visitors Center
Bldg. 1200
Stennis Space Center, MS 39529-6000
Admission free.
9 AM - 5 PM
Seven days
(601) 688-2370

HOW TO GO:

I-10 east to Mississippi. Take exit 2 and follow Hwy. 607 north to the entrance gate.

NASA introduces visitors to highlights of the space program, scientific innovations from outer space, live rocket engine testing, and a commemorative art collection at Stennis Space Center in Mississippi.

engines ignite. The steam, flames, and roar can last as long as 30 minutes during engine testing.

Even without the drama of engine testing, the colorful tri-level visitor center is worth the trip. Three decades of space program history and some future plans are showcased in exhibits that include "home" movies by the astronauts and NASA's documentary art collection. From medicine to weather forecasting, the applications of space research are explained in layman's language. Other displays describe the connection between the Navy's Oceanographic Command, the National Data Buoy Center, the National Marine Fisheries Service, the U.S. Geological Survey, and other organizations who now rent portions of the base.

Despite space program cutbacks, the facility's usefulness has been assured by the ongoing space shuttle program and by sharing the once exclusively NASA-operated facility with other scientific and technological enterprises.

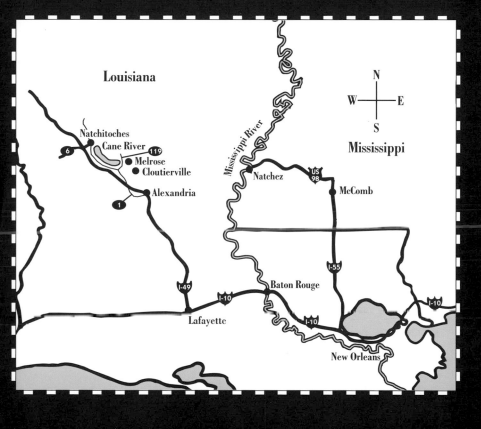

Melrose Plantation
and Bayou Folk Museum

PIONEERING WOMEN
SHAPED LOUISIANA
CULTURE

WITHIN 3 to 4 HOURS

HOW TO GO:
I-10 to Lafayette. I-49 north through Alexandria, east on LA 119 at Derry. Follow LA 119 north to Melrose; or follow Hwy. 1 south and Hwy. 491 east to Cloutierville. Kate Chopin's home is called the Bayou Folk Museum. Another plantation open for visitors along Hwy. 119 is Magnolia, south of Melrose.

MELROSE PLANTATION
Tour Chairman
P.O. Box 2248
Natchitoches, LA 71457
By admission: $
(318) 379-0055

I went to Cane River Country for its pastoral views and relaxing country pace and discovered four dynamic women who once lived there—a writer, a painter, an art patron, and an eighteenth-century black woman who owned one of the area's largest plantations. Following the road to Melrose Plantation—where three of the women once lived—I saw tractors dragging plows and clouds of red dust through fallow fields. Fine crops of cotton, sorghum, and sugarcane filled nearby fields. New homes along Cane River Lake faced rustic farm buildings and sleepy long-horned cattle. Just before Melrose Plantation, I drove into the shade of a pecan grove that stretched for miles like a giant tent of spreading limbs poised on fat, geometrically spaced pecan trunks.

Melrose Plantation was once the property of Marie Therese Coin Coin, an African slave who worked for the French soldiers in Natchitoches' Fort St. John Baptiste in the 1760s. She had seven children with French soldier Thomas Pierre Metoyer and upon the dissolution of their relationship was given six acres of land and her freedom. Over the next 30 years Coin Coin purchased the freedom of her seven children, expanded the six acres to 11,000 acres and became a slave owner herself. Coin Coin's son built the often-photographed African House at Melrose Plantation—the only Congo-style architecture in Louisiana—to honor his mother's African origins.

Since Coin Coin's era, Melrose Plantation has changed. Today a colonial-style main house is flanked by twin garconniéres built in the early twentieth century when it was home to patron of the arts, Cammie Henry. Small cabins that housed writers, painters, and weavers are scattered among the African-style buildings and plantation gardens. Among Henry's more notable visiting

Under the eaves at the African House on Melrose Plantation. Clementine Hunter's paintings hang in a gallery on the second floor.

artists were William Faulkner and John Steinbeck.

Clementine Hunter, a former field hand, worked as Henry's cook. In her early fifties Hunter began painting, using discarded tubes of paint left by resident artists. Encouraged by Henry and her visitors, Hunter created hundreds of paintings and gained a national reputation as a folk artist. Her fame even brought the world of art thieves to quiet Cane River Country: $150,000 of Hunter's paintings were stolen from a Natchitoches gallery in 1990.

Current-less Cane River Lake, a 32-mile river fragment, mirrors riverside homes in old Natchitoches.

Several paintings are displayed in African House which has been turned into a gallery for Hunter's work. Visitors can also tour the plantation's great house, weaving cabin, and chapel.

Kate Chopin's former home, a two-story brick and cedar cottage in the nearby town of Cloutierville, was disappointing to me, a reader of her vivid fiction. It was filled with local antiques, but little related to Chopin except a few books on sale. Chopin spent much more time in New Orleans than in Cloutierville, the small country town which was home to her husband's banking and mercantile family. When her husband lost his city job in 1879, she and her children moved to Cloutierville where they took charge of the family plantation and general store until his untimely death in 1882. Eventually Kate Chopin returned to her family home in St. Louis and began to write the stories of liberated womanhood that shocked Victorian America.

There was a time when Kate Chopin's *The Awakening* was banned from public libraries, and when no one would encourage a cook like Clementine Hunter to take up painting. However, the efforts of these Cane River women have opened doors used daily by contemporary women.

GOOD TIMES TO GO:

During the Natchitoches Pilgrimage in October, the plantation tour ticket lets you visit Melrose, Magnolia, Cherokee (not usually open for tours), and the Bayou Folk Museum. There is also a Town Tour of historic Natchitoches and a Candlelight Tour. Call the Natchitoches Parish Tourist Commission (800) 959-1714 for further information.

BAYOU FOLK MUSEUM

Cloutierville, LA 71416
P.O. Box 411
Natchitoches, LA 71457
(800) 259-1714
By admission: $
For information call:
Natchitoches Chamber of Commerce

Tractors are a regular part of the landscape in Cane River Country.

Historic House Tours

SMALL TOWN WITH BIG HOUSES A HIT WITH HISTORY BUFFS

HOW TO GO:

I-10 to I-55 north across the Mississippi border to McComb. Turn west on U.S. 98 until it joins U.S. 84. Just outside Natchez turn onto U.S. 61 & 84, the belt highway, and follow it until U.S. 61 drops off. Continue on U.S. 84 until just before the Mississippi River Bridge. Turn into old Natchez on S. Canal Street.

BEST TIME TO GO:

Fall and spring Pilgrimages in October and March feature house tour packages and costumed guides. Call for information and reservations on all year-round tourist events.

NATCHEZ PILGRIMAGE TOURS CANAL AT STATE STREET

P.O. Box 347
Natchez, MS 39121
(800) 647-6742

Though it makes a very long day trip from New Orleans, Natchez is essential to include in this book because of its extraordinary wealth of historic properties and strong ties to the Crescent City. Families, river trade, and architecture link the two cities, and with over 500 historic properties to explore, Natchez can entertain a visitor for days. A highway that encircles the town has attracted most modern businesses to the outskirts, leaving the old center of town with few shops and little nightlife. But for those who seek quiet and relaxation, the restorative charms of Natchez come from its slow pace, gardens, and river views.

In Natchez, which is built on bluffs overlooking the Mississippi River, birdsong fills the air in the parks and gardens around the town. While visiting the hilltop gardens at The Briars—a historic planter's home, now an exclusive bed and breakfast—I realized why there were so many birds. Natchez sits on the highest point for miles around. The birds, carried by wind currents along the Mississippi River, stop and rest their weary wings in the safety of plantation woods and gardens before continuing on.

If you arrive at The Briars with ruffled feathers, they will be smoothed by the time you leave. Located on a private road behind a busy Ramada Inn, guests at The Briars can roam acres of landscaped gardens punctuated by animal topiary, European sculpture, and sweeping river views. Accommodations are in either a modern, comfortable building near a pool and tennis courts, or in the main house, an early nineteenth-century plantation home where Jefferson Davis was married. The parlors and galleries of the main house are accessible to all guests and worth studying for their architectural details. Gracefully proportioned wooden planes make up the Federal style mantels. The wide arches and door mouldings are handcarved.

There are so many historic properties worth seeing in Natchez, it's hard to decide which to see first. My hosts at The Briars were helpful. "Well it's hard to choose. But you must see Rosalie, Lansdowne, Stanton Hall, and Melrose," said owners, Newton Wilds and Bob Canon.

Each place had its virtues: Rosalie because it was the model for many of the white-columned mansions in the South; Lansdowne with its original Rococo Revival furnishings and wallpaper; Stanton Hall for sheer size and impressiveness, and Melrose because it is run by the park service and has an estate setting that includes outbuildings. They are all more properly termed "suburban estates" rather than plantation homes because their owners chose to live in Natchez, while owning plantations some distance away.

You will find your own favorites among Natchez historic homes. Some tours, like Lansdowne, are conducted by family members who live in the house. Others are large landscaped properties, carefully tended by the ladies of Natchez's ever-prominent garden clubs.

One house that should not be missed is Longwood—a remarkable 30,000 square foot octagonal house whose construction was interrupted by the Civil War. The upper floors remained incomplete, while the descendants lived in near-poverty on the first floor until 1970 when it was turned over to the Pilgrimage Garden Club.

In between house tours I took two open-air, unguided visits to historic burial grounds in Natchez. One was the town cemetery and the other, the Grand Village of the Natchez Indians. Both are well worth the time.

The Grand Village, a National Historic Landmark located on the outskirts of Natchez, consists of an interpretive center with displays on the Natchez Indians, several large mounds, a nature trail, and a replica of an Indian house. The Natchez chiefs lived atop the mounds overlooking the village below. Walking in a big grassy space between mounds reminds you of the Indians that inhabited the area until the arrival of the Europeans.

Though it was a remarkable culture, I didn't envy the life of a Natchez Indian chieftain's wife. First of all, the chief's wife was not noble. If she bore children, *they* were noble, but according to the rules, the chief, or Sun, could only marry from the common people called "stinkards." When the Sun died his stinkard wife and retainers were strangled so they could accompany him into the next life. Then the Sun's house and everyone in it were burned and covered over. A new Sun built his house on top, hence the mounds.

Unlike New Orleanians, today's Natchezians bury their dead below ground. The Natchez cemetery is remarkable for its beautiful wrought iron fences, lovely monuments, and perfectly kept greenery. "When the cemetery was turned over to the Natchez Cemetery Association in 1908, it was the city's first example of preservation," said historian Randolph Delehanty.

In the cemetery is a large Jewish section that dates back to a time when many Eastern European Jews worked the trades in the flourishing river town. Later I saw Clifton Heights, a residential area where rows of handsome Victorian homes were built by these merchants. Their synagogue, Temple B'nai Israel, is a 1904 Beaux Art

The interior of Longwood was never finished above the first floor. The Civil War interrupted construction and impoverished the owners of this remarkable octagonal structure. For the next 100 years descendants of the builder lived on the first floor.

style building downtown. The present Jewish population is so small it requested that the Museum of the Southern Jewish Experience in Jackson insure the temple's preservation. An exhibit area, public programs, and lectures are planned.

Near the synagogue is Trinity Episcopal Church, noteworthy both for its architecture and its two breathtaking Tiffany windows. Inspired by the Greek Temple Thesion, the church has a serene golden interior with contrasting dark wooden beams. On the left as you face the altar, Tiffany's Angel of Resurrection is worth a close look. Inch-thick undulating glass, dotted with glass "jewels" and an iridescent sky, resemble the topography of a mountain range.

When Jefferson Davis married at The Briars it was a suburban estate, set apart from town on the Natchez Bluffs. Today an exclusive bed and breakfast, The Briars remains secluded among topiary and sculpture-studded gardens.

Downtown is the office of the Historic Natchez Foundation with samples of reproduction furniture, wallpaper, fabric, lamps, and jewelry copied from the antiques found in Natchez houses. Though the Foundation does not sell the pieces, they fund their programs from royalties received from use of these designs. Manufacturing firms from all over the country reproduce these items and the Foundation can direct you to the appropriate retailer. "We call them reproductions and adaptations because people today desire a higher chair seat than in the 1850s. Also some pieces like coffee tables didn't exist then," said Mary Warren Miller, architectural historian with the foundation.

After so much touring, I was interested in a good, relaxing meal. Dinner at Liza's Restaurant was a perfect way to end a long day touring other people's houses. It too is in an old house, but a very intimate one. The restaurant is casual and friendly but the food rivals restaurants that make their names with sky-high prices and pretentious service. Another choice is Gallaghers, housed in an old bank building on Main Street. For travellers from New Orleans longing for a taste of home, both restaurants specialize in New Orleans-inspired cuisine.

Historic City on Cane River

More than a century ago Natchitoches, Louisiana was on the fast track of river-town expansion when a log jam turned the course of the Red River to Shreveport, derailing development, and preserving the town's nineteenth-century facade. What must have been an economic tragedy at the time is a happy accident for today's travelers. Creole cottages and pillared mansions fill a 30-block square historic district: the only National Historic Landmark district in Louisiana outside of New Orleans' French Quarter. The town sits beside Cane River Lake, a 32-mile river fragment where anglers, water-skiers, rowers, and tour boats find plenty of elbow room.

Under the moss-hung live oaks of the historic district I found a few good restaurants, antique stores, a local artist worth collecting, and bed and breakfasts where proprietors share family history and the folklore of Cane River Country. Often crowded with tourists, Natchitoches is experiencing a boom of sorts: the movie *Steel Magnolias* was filmed there, tourism is on the rise, and the current-free Cane River Lake is used regularly for college rowing events and bass tournaments. Opportunities for touring Old Natchitoches are plentiful. There are motorized "trolley" tours, walking tours, waterfront tours, and even video tours. Oddly enough all this doesn't add up to a "touristy" feeling, but rather a plentiful package of choices for exploring Natchitoches in your own style.

The historic district is large enough to feel like a real neighborhood, but easily walkable and made up of many small, intimately scaled homes with neatly kept gardens. Drivers waved hello as I wandered down the streets looking for original bousillage (fortified mud) construction. To beat the heat, I rested on a wrought iron bench overlooking the waterfront. I chatted with strolling families and watched returning water-skiers skirt a flotilla of swans.

Everything about Natchitoches except the name (pronounced nak-i-tush) seemed easy and accessible. The hostess of the first restaurant I visited, The Landing on Front Street, suggested I tour the town with "this real character who knows everything about the town and who happens to be my mama." One phone call and she'd arranged a *rendezvous* at Lasyone's, home of Natchitoches' famous meat pies.

LOUISIANA'S OLDEST TOWN BOASTS WATER SPORTS, HISTORIC HOUSES, AND FAMOUS MEAT PIES

WITHIN 3 to 4 HOURS

HOW TO GO:
I-10 to Lafayette, then I-49 north through Alexandria to Hwy. 6. Go east to Natchitoches. The Historic Landmark District is on the west bank of Cane River Lake.

SPECIAL TIMES TO GO:
Natchitoches Pilgrimage in October. Candlelight Tour, Town Tour, and Cane River Country Tour include properties normally closed to the public. During December's Festival of the Lights, thousands of tiny white Christmas lights fill Cane River Lake with twinkling reflections. Call for further information.

Natchitoches has the largest historic district in Louisiana outside the French Quarter in New Orleans.

NATCHITOCHES PARISH TOURIST COMMISSION

Dept. B
P.O. Box 411
Natchitoches, LA 71458
(800) 259-1714

Natchitoches, as seen through the eyes of tour guide Lori Tate, was a tantalizing jumble of ancient and recent events: "This town, founded in 1714, is the oldest permanent European settlement in the Louisiana Purchase. And that, right over there is where I had my big crying scene as mother of the groom," she said. Tate who sports unusual eyeglasses from 1956, appeared thirteen times in *Steel Magnolias*. She drives a pink car with a license plate reading "Yes. I AM A MOVIE STAR."

I followed Tate's high-heeled pink shoes up and down stairways all over town, peering into basement hideaways for the Underground Railroad, meeting store owners, and dashing through historic houses. I didn't allow nearly enough time for Tate's tour. Among places that deserve a longer look were Cloutier Town House, a beautifully appointed bed and breakfast in Ducournau Square; Just Friends Restaurant, favorite dining spot for the *Steel Magnolias* crew; historic Fort Jean Baptiste, recreated in the manner and construction methods of 1733; Prudhomme Rouquier House, and several other houses which open for Natchitoches' annual Pilgrimage in October.

After I left Tate, I stopped at the Natchitoches Genealogical and Historical Association, located in the old Courthouse on Second Street where Tate said they used to hang convicts in the stairwell. Members of the staff who were helping a visitor from Texas trace his roots through Natchitoches back to France said they'd never heard of the stairwell hangings. "It's not surprising though. There are so many unusual characters in our past."

Index